'DEAR DAUGHTER'

THE MESSENGER LETTERS

Captain Thomas Messenger

'DEAR DAUGHTER'

THE MESSENGER LETTERS

Voyages of a Sailing Ship Captain 1890-1898.

Edited and Introduced
by Graham Hindle

JOHN GRAY BOOKS

Published and distributed by:
John Gray Books,
39 Moorland Road, Langho, Blackburn, Lancashire BB6 8HA

ISBN 0 9534609 0 8

British Library Cataloguing in Publication Data:
a catalogue record for this book is available from the British Library.

Production and typesetting:
Dick Richardson, Country Books, Little Longstone DE45 1NN

Printed by:
MFP Design & Print, Manchester M32 0JT

Bound by:
Cedric Chivers Ltd, Longwell Green, Bristol

PREFACE

Describing the voyages of Tom Messenger, one of the last of the sailing ship Skippers, these diaries are a fascinating and invaluable record; an insight into a period a mere 100 years ago, which may as well be a 100 light years in terms of social and scientific change.

Captain Messenger did not have the benefit of steam power and was writing just before Marconi's marvellous invention and all its derivatives. No radio, radar, sonar devices, satellite or other navigation aids now taken for granted and before the Panama canal was opened.

The unsung heroism is remarkable, even if it was his job; people like Captain Messenger played a major role in laying the foundations of today's world.

Regularly negotiating Cape Horn, traversing the iceberg-littered, fog-bound Southern Ocean, hitting submerged rocks, electrical storms and displays of the Southern Lights, 60 feet long sea snakes, whales the width of the ship and catching sharks with a lump of pork were part of a day's work.

Yet these letters also captivate on another level. I always imagined sailing ship Captains of that era as being in the mould of Bligh of the Bounty. Yet throughout this saga the humanity and humour of the man are obvious. Through every vicissitude, he remains generally philosphical but realistic, displaying considerable fatherly concern for a tough old seadog, towards his crew as well as his daughter.

Nevertheless at times there is the definite impression that writing the letters was therapeutic, helping to keep his mind on an 'even keel'; alleviating frustration, loneliness and danger.

1998 is the centenary of the cessation of the letters; a fitting time to offer them to a wider audience.

INTRODUCTION

I feel both fortunate and privileged that fate enabled me to become involved with the Messenger letters. The reader may appreciate a little background as to how this came about.

I was born and raised in the small Cumbrian coastal town of Maryport which, until World War 1, had a seafaring reputation disproportionate to to its size (current pop. 10,000 approx.) and location. Indeed at one time it handled more tonnage than Liverpool. The main industries were coal and iron-ore mining, iron and steel making and building and servicing ships. The area also bred a race of hardy seafaring men; among them was Thomas Messenger.

He had one daughter, Mary Adelaide, who became a teacher and remained a spinster. As a child in the village of Crosby, about two miles from Maryport, she was a friend of my mother's aunt. Aunt Esther was like a second mother to me, living with us as part of the family. Our house was large and we rented out one floor as a flat.

When Miss Messenger retired, aunt must have had a hand in her being offered the flat. Through my father's great interest in them, I became aware of the letters and their significance. When Mary Adelaide died, father became custodian of the letters. I remember him being in correspondence with the letters column of the Guardian, learning that the Dunboyne, which Tom Messenger sailed in as Mate, was situated in Copenhagen harbour in the 1950s; it had been used as a sail training ship in Scandinavia. From recent correspondence, I find that it is still in use there as a Youth Hostel, 110 years after its launch (Appendix C).

In due time I inherited the letters and, although some have been published previously as extracts, it has long been my ambition to transcribe them fully for posterity. The original intention was to do so for the Cumbrian Archives but I also felt that a wider public should have access to them.

I have resisted the temptation to interject exclamation marks at every twinkle in the man's eye; the script would have been littered with them. I have tried to keep as far as possible to the original, but the reader will certainly appreciate what is going on his mind. You can almost see the wry smile on his face at times. He writes conversationally and tends to ramble a little; so I must take responsibility for some of the punctuation. He was obviously an educated man but his syntax is a little unusual; nevertheless I have tried to retain the character of the manuscript. Occasional Cumbrian or Northern colloquialisms occur.

A few facts to set the scene for some of his comments. His wife, whom he greatly missed, had died when Mary Adelaide was very young and she lived with relatives. The letters cover 8 years, during which time he progressed from Mate of the Dunboyne to Captain, first of the newly-built Ladas (named after a Derby winner) and later the Midas. On later travels, nephew Willie was a crew member. The correspondence started when Mary was about eight and able to appreciate his letters and travels, continuing until the unfortunate and dramatic events of 1898, when she would be about 16. At that time she was an apprentice teacher. Some of his voyages lasted up to 2 years, with approximately two months between trips. Although it is a remarkably complete record, there appear to be one or two minor gaps. Also the dating is a little erratic at times; I hope the reader will make allowances for these apparent discrepancies.

A definite change in tone can be noted in his letters as mate to those after becoming captain. He almost seemed happier when more active, although physically the life was taking its toll.

There is frequent mention of captain and crew going to church although he never made them do so. It is apparent that the Messengers were more chapel than church, but his daughter had to start attending the C of E Sunday School, as she had ambitions to become a teacher in schools run by the established church.

The ships were owned by Mr Ritson, a Maryport businessman. The vessels were constructed in West Cumbria and those built at Maryport were launched broadside because the river was so narrow, sometimes in full sail. My aunt used to say that the schoolchildren were given a holiday and many who gathered on the opposite hillside was soaked by the big splash. Mr Ritson's early death is mentioned in the letters but I knew of the family because his sisters survived him by many years and my mother was their hairdresser, visiting them in their mansion on the outskirts of town, now a hotel.

Newspaper cuttings and old photographs accompany the letters,

7

mainly of the family, his ships and crews, but there are also one or two of Nagasaki nearly 50 years before the atom bomb. Interestingly, these are coloured, presumably by tinting.

A short appendix is also included about the career of Tom Messenger's friend Captain Walker, also from West Cumbria, who was influential in the setting up of the Mitsubishi Corporation.

Some of the content is mundane. Often he had a tedious wait for unloading and loading in remote corners of the world. Yet the need to write reguarly to his daughter seemed to sharpen his observation, providing an insight into the early development of many places throughout the world. Vancouver for instance, now a city of 1,500,000, had a population of only 23,000 in the 1890's. Routine matters such as keeping his clothes washed and repaired was a major problem in rough weather for days on end; yet it is nature and the marine environment which provide the moments of high drama

The overall picture which emerges is indeed amazing.

J Graham Hindle
Blackburn
August 1998

CONTENTS

Voyages as Master of Barque Midas.

APPENDICES

U.K. TO PORT PIRIE, AUSTRALIA, 1891

Ship Dunboyne, Off Beachy Head.   *August 1891.*

My Dear Daughter,
I hope you got back on shore all right and the tugboat did not make you sea sick. We have had it very fine since we left but a good deal of foul winds and now we have it right dead against us.

The Captain's wife is not sea sick but feels queer and looks very white but I hope she will soon get used to it (the sea I mean) and get well again. I suppose you will be at home again now and ready to start school again tomorrow. Then you must make up for lost time. I hope H.E. has not lost all her customers by being away so long.

My room is beginning to want tidying up a bit again and my towel wants washing.

That strong breeze we had did not last long; the ship soon ran out of it. It may be some days before the pilot will leave us yet, as the wind is so far ahead and he is going a long way down with us; but we may get a fair wind soon and then he won't go so far.

I hope you managed to get to the station all right and in good time after you got on shore. You can say you have been to see a big ship sail and set her on her way a little bit. You must write out to The Ship Dunboyne, Port Pirie, South Australia, 6 weeks after you get this. I reckon on being about 90 days going out. So with love to yourself, Aunt Jane and all next door, I remain, Your Brother and Father,   *T. Messenger.*

Tuesday. Off Torbay and the Pilot will be leaving soon. With love to all, Goodbye.

Ship Dunboyne   *S.E.Trades. Lat.17S Long. 36W*

My Dear Daughter,
I just think I will write you a few lines to let you know how well we

The Ship Dunboyne. Built Whitehaven 1888. 1,450 gross tonnage

are getting on, or rather how badly we get on I should say. So far, we have done only moderately well but as we have had very fine weather all the time except the first few days after we left Barry, we cannot grumble. It is nearly a calm now and, in a calm, we lay just like 'a painted ship upon a painted ocean'. Writing of painting, we have been very busy at that this week; everything painted over, all spick and span and if Aunt Lizzie's house were here, I could paint that for her well.

I was using some of the thread you got me in Sunderland, mending my inexpressibles the other night and I fancied I did it very well. You see I am so very poor I can not buy new ones, or at any rate neglected to do so in Barry.

Everyone is all well and the baby is growing fast the Captain is a first rate nurse. As it is evening, the sailors are all busy singing songs forward and making a noise generally. I have just been hanging up that pipe rack the old Carpenter made me but I will have to borrow a pipe or two to put in it.

The lamp is making my head bad, so good night.   *T.M.*

Sat Oct. 1st. 8pm.
I have just been mending my old stockings to put on and searching out other old clothes to give to a stowaway from Barry. How generous we are with things we have no more use for or are tired of. It is blowing quite a strong gale and has been for two days but as we are travelling some 250 miles daily, we don't mind it. We are getting in the vicinity of some Islands and it is generally more or less dirty around them and we get no sun and so do not know where we are for certain.

Monday Oct. 3rd.
Just been sewing on some buttons on an old jacket and trimming up for the cold weather which we are getting into now. Passed the island at 2 o'clock this morning (Gough Island). Can you find it on the map? Still a fine breeze. Just a little more than halfway out to Port Pirie

Thursday 6th
Today it is quite calm and sunny, the first sunny day we have had

for some time. All our chickens are out, seeming to enjoy it as much as I do myself after the last two days cold we have had. Miss O'Neill (baby) is growing very fast but this morning she was very cross; drove the Captain on deck before 5 o'clock with her crying. So he was telling Mrs O'Neill they would have to keep watch and watch to keep the baby quiet and he would nurse it in the forenoon. So they are all keeping watch asleep. It is now a dead calm; consequently we lay just like a painted ship upon a painted ocean. Only we have some life around us; lots of Cape pidgeons, albatross, mollyhawks and Cape hens, also a few gulls and Mother Carey's chickens (stormy petrels). I hope we will soon get a breeze again and go on our way rejoicing but there is time enough to grumble yet.

Sunday 9th.
Now we have a strong breeze driving the ship along at 14 mile an hour and we passed the meridian of the Cape of Good Hope today, 87 days out, a fairly good passage so far. The ship was throwing a fair amount of water on board today and I saw the Bosun (Boatswain) get a good baptising this forenoon. I got a little myself too but not so much, I kept out of the way. I see that from here to Port Pirie last voyage we were just 27 days; if we do it in the same time we will have made a good passage. Baby O'N. is growing fast and she does like sugar and water. Mrs gives it a tit dipped in that to keep her quiet and she won't be quiet long without it. All our hens have stopped laying eggs and we can't get any now as we are not near a market town.   So good night my dear.

Tuesday Night 11th.
Still we carry on a strong favourable wind but just a little cold and disagreeable last night and the ship lying over on her broadside. One can hardly stand on deck and it makes it bad to get the sail of the ship without reckoning the seas coming on board likely to knock one down. Fortunately we are so light we have very little of it coming on deck, though some of the men were knocked down today. We could just see a ship away in the distance this afternoon, apparently coming upon us. A long while since we saw one before. So goodnight, it is 8 o'clock and I must go on deck until 12.

Monday 17th.

We have been going fast for this last week and are keeping up 260 miles a day or thereabouts. Last night we passed another vessel very fast, or rather we could only see his lights for about an hour and the ship was not in sight today

Wednesday, 19th.

Just got fine weather again after a very heavy storm and sea most mountainous. The ship did tumble about a lot and set everything rolling. Knocked a molasses cask to pieces and all the molasses got amongst the potatoes and made a fine mess. Washed the 'taties' clean and they did want cleaning badly, as they were getting rotten. We only have few potatoes left now after throwing all the bad ones overboard. Not enough left to carry us out to Port Pirie. The steward's leg is bad so we have boy in the cabin. He is a bit better today; the loss of his molasses stirred him up a bit. I had to wash a section of my towel again tonight after washing myself; I can't keep enough water in the basin to wash half, so just washed a small part this time. One can only hold on to get a wash every two or three days. I don't know how the Mrs. manages with baby but she is thriving immensely. She is getting forward enough to put things into her mouth now.

Tuesday October 25th.

We have had a very fine day today and made the best distance for a long time (130 miles). The last few days we had very stormy weather. On Sunday we were tumbling about in all directions and blew away the foresail. Couldn't get my face washed. Hope to get out in ten days more if we are moderately fortunate. Steward's leg is still bad; he does not make any toffee now.

Thursday 27th.

A very strong breeze today to make up for the last two days fine weather and I daresay it will be dirty and raining tonight. The ship is laying on her broadside almost and we can hardly stand on the deck. Stewards leg is no better. I washed another section of my towel today; it takes two days to dry. Baby is well.

15

Friday 28th.
We did have a stormy rainy day of it today and tumbled about a good deal and got wet with both salt and fresh water, but after 4 o'clock the sun came out and dried us up a little. Now it is a fine clear night, 8 pm and I am going to turn into bed. This last watch or two, I have been sleeping on the edge of the bunk board and my back is sore. Goodnight.

Sunday 30th.
Another stormy day again, ship pitching water clean over the fore end, but it is clear and sun shining and we are going along the right road so we don't grumble, though we can hardly stand on our feet. The baby has the best of this weather; the ship swings the cot for her.

Wednesday Noon. Latitude 37S Longitude 132E.
Just about 190 miles from Cape Bordon, but our fine breeze has died away and what is left is drawing ahead. So we will not get to the land tomorrow, but I hope we will get to Port by Saturday. The weather is getting warm and I have taken my stockings off today as we were doing some scrubbing and washing. Steward's leg is bad still and he is lying up nursing it. For myself, I never was better. I feel I must be growing young again, for which blessing I am truly thankful. You can tell Tom I will bring him a knife with a hole in it this time, as he will be a big lad by I get back home again.

Friday Evening
Now we are in the Gulf. Passed Kangaroo Island at 5 o'clock with a nice fair wind and have 160 miles to go yet, but hope to be up tomorrow night or afternoon perhaps and we have made a very good passage. We have some company going up, another vessel, the South Esk and one going in for Port Adelaide. Every one of our men seem to have got the itch; one of the lads is broken out all over his body and legs and they almost make me itch to see them scratching themselves.

Sunday November 6th.

Anchored here last night at 8 o'clock and so far have made the best passage of the season. They would not allow anyone to come on board or leave the ship until the doctor had granted permission; they are very much afraid of cholera from Europe now. We had the doctor and his wife on board this afternoon. They are old friends of Mrs O'Neill from last voyage. It is about 7 or 8 miles up to Port Pirie from where we are lying and they say we have to lay here for a week or ten days before we can get a berth at the wharf. It will be much cooler out here and we can keep the men on board and get some work done. They tell me here they are just going to commence to reap tomorrow and there is going to be plenty of wheat this year. So we will likely load here again. I hear that the Captain of the ship which left Barry before us died a few days before she arrived here. He was an old man. It is a chance if any of your letters will have come yet, but I hope you are all well at home and you are getting on with your schooling well.

Dear Jane,

We have arrived all well after a fairly good passage of 84 days and we expect to load here for home. I am glad to say that I have been very well all the way out and I hope that you are keeping clear of the cholera as I hear it has been bad at Hamburg.

With love to all, I remain your brother,   *T. Messenger*

Dunboyne, Port Pirie.   *Sunday November 11th 1891.*

My Dear Daughter,

Your letter came safe to hand and I am glad to see that you are quite well. I think you and Aunt Jane would feel lonely after H.M. and the children went away.

We have only just got clear of the coke yet and still have the coals to put out. As we are going to load here, we may still be some time before we get that out and will likely be here for another month yet.

We had a very wild and stormy night last night and it has been windy all day today. I got to the Wesleyan chapel this morning but have not been on shore tonight. Last night there was a concert at the

17

Reading Rooms here. Mostly sailors from the ships were singing and it was well attended. They are getting up a kind of Sailor's Rest by the Women's Christian Temperance League and they can't manage to make it pay expenses, though many of the leading ladies of the place are in it and were singing last night. I did not go and sing any myself last night.

I may be home in time for your holidays this next year if we are not too soon. Christmas will soon be here and all kinds of sports and excursions are advertised from this place. We are wondering if they are going to send us to Wallaroo for New Year's Day again. We don't mind if they do, it is quite gay on that day.

There is a silver refinery here close alongside and they say they have £30,000 (Thirty thousand pounds) of silver ready stacked for shipment. It will go to Adelaide by rail and from there home by the Mail. We can go through the works and see them make the silver right from the ore. First the bullion, then the lead, then zinc and antimony and finally silver. The other stuff is sent home and they get gold from it.

Our Steward is still on shore but his leg is a great deal better and he will be soon coming to the ship again. Mrs. O'Neill and baby are both well. It is a good baby that never cries at all and likes to be out on deck to see what is going on.

With love I remain your Father, *T. Messenger.*

Port Pirie, *Mon. Nov. 16th 1891.*

My Dear Daughter,
I am pleased to say that we arrived safe here last Friday after a passage of 92 days and we have made better than our neighbours as some very long passages have been made. We have beat the General Roberts by 6 days, that's the ship which sailed the day after we came down to Sunderland. They have put us alongside of them here to wait for a day or two, while they get a clear berth for us to discharge at.

I am pleased to say that I have been very well all the time, but just before getting in here, my nose played me a mean trick by breaking out and getting all scabbed again; and the backs of my ears likewise, but they are nearly better now.

I had a small walk round the town yesterday; it is a very small town and did not take long to get around. Most of the working people are living in tents, evidently made of old bags and I noticed their chimneys were all made of old kerosene tins nailed one above the other and no doubt it answers very well for a good time.

I have received all the letters I suppose as I had four all at once but not a newspaper. I was glad to see you got away all right and in good time from Sunderland, but you don't say whether the tug-boat made you sick going back on shore or not.

The Captain's wife is very good, she does not keep us awake much playing the piano. When she does play, it is very softly. She is not one of the 'Thump the grand piano' sort. I think she was very tired of being at sea when we arrived. She did not have much sea sickness but was sick for a while.

We have no idea where we are going from here, but I am afraid it will be across San Francisco way by Newcastle or Sydney. The mail leaves tomorrow and I will not have time to write to Aunt Lizzie, so tell her I got her letter and will write next week when I will probably know where we are going to. Steward says we are going to have some rhubarb tomorrow and he will make you some toffee when we come home.

With love to yourself, Aunt Jane and all at the Moor, I am your father, *T. Messenger.*

Ship Dunboyne, Port Pirie,   *December 8th 1891.*

My Dear Daughter,
Your letters safely received and very pleased to see you are so well and I am so likewise. At least we know what we are going to do with the ship; we are going to get part cargo of wheat here and complete remainder at Wallaroo, a place some 40 miles down the Gulf here. Then proceed to Queenstown or Falmouth most likely. We have got rid of all our coke but still have the pig iron in and don't know when we will get rid of it. Christmas will soon be here and I hope you will all be well enough to enjoy it at Crosby. It is likely to be very hot here as it is their Summer and

they are just cutting their corn. I can see cornfields about here at the foot of the hills but the harvest is very poor I believe. However no doubt they will have enough corn to load us and send us home rejoicing. This will be only a short voyage, 8 or 9 months at most, so I will be back in summer time again; should be home in May sometime. This is a wretched place for having to move the ship about, we are never sure of having a full days quietness. I have not much time to write more to you by this mail.

The Salvation Army is the only excitement to be had here; last Sunday they had a grand band here and had a very lively time of it. I got nearly melted in Hall at night it was so crowded, nearly a 1000 people were there.

Much love to all, I conclude,   *T. Messenger.*

The crew of the Dunboyne

PORT PIRIE TO QUEENSTOWN 1892

Ship Dunboyne, Port Pirie.   *Jan 22nd 1892.*

My dear Daughter,
You will be looking long for a letter from me as I have been very lazy in the last month and not written to you. Now we are outside, ready for sea and will leave on Tuesday I daresay. We had to move out of the Port this Sunday morning for fear of not getting out for a week if the tides should fall lower. So we started at 8 o clock and got out of here by half past ten.

Of course we are all very glad to get away out of this place again and I do hope we shall have a good journey home. They say we are either going to Dublin or London. Of the two I prefer London, but we will know tomorrow when the Captain comes.

Three boys from a ship in the Port came all the way out in their boat. They rowed out some 10 miles I suppose and as a strong breeze came on, they were waiting for it to die down before starting back. But about 4 o' clock their boat got adrift and was going away for the beach before anyone noticed her. So I had to send our boat after her with some of our lads to help them, but they could not pull back to the ship so they have gone into Port here about 3 miles away. They will have to stay there all night as it is blowing hard still. They will have had enough pulling for sometime I should think.

I see by the papers you have had some hard frost again this Winter and that London river has been frozen over. Mrs O'Neill and baby are stopping on shore until the Captain comes tomorrow or Thursday. Baby has grown fat and strong since we came in here and she can wave her hand and say 'Ta'. So the Mrs. is very proud showing her off. The Steward says its over far to send a lump of toffee for you so he can only send his love. I hope you are quite well at home and also at Crosby and with kind love I conclude, from your loving Father,

                    T. Messenger.

Ship Dunboyne, Wallaroo.   *Friday. (1892).*

At last we are ready for sea and hope to get away in the morning, as we have got all our sailors on board and sobered. Yesterday we had the ship crowded with visitors, who primarily came to see a Man of War here called the Katoomba. They seemed to know she was coming, as the people came in on the trains from all round, just the same as they did on New Year's Day. There was far more wind yesterday; in fact it was quite rough and many of them got wet going back.

We are very glad to get away from this, although on the whole we have had a very good time in Wallaroo. Or I should say the boys have. Plenty of young girls for them here; brass buttons and peak caps go a long way amongst them, or it seems so by the way they come down to the ship after them. I tell them what I have missed by not being young and good looking myself. Another vessel came in yesterday so the pier will not be left bare when we go, though she is only a small Barque. I see the Captain has his wife on board also.

I do not expect to be much over 100 days coming home, but it is quite possible we may be and we have 7 days to wait for orders at Falmouth or Queenstown. Here is a card I have just had from Port Pirie. A kind friend there remembered us all and sent each one a card, to our very great surprise. I hope they do not send us on to the Continent to discharge our cargo; you see it is so far away from home.

Sunday Jan. 17th.

We have made a little start towards getting away, as we left the wharf and came out to the Bay yesterday. I think we will make a start some time tomorrow, if the wind will let us.

The Steward has got a very fine parrot; it whistles lots of tunes and has a very knowing look. We have also a kangaroo on board, a young one. It does not talk or whistle but it is very tame; it belongs to the Captain. There are a couple of pups and lots of chickens, so we have quite a family party on board.

With kind love to you and Aunt Jane and the rest at the Moor. I remain your loving Father,

T. Messenger.

23

Ship Dunboyne, Seattle.   *February 1ᵦ.*

My Dear Daughter,

I have received your letter in answer to my first one and I am very pleased to see that you are all very well at Crosby. Well we ought to have been away from here a fortnight ago, but we had to pull aside and let some other ships get loaded first and I hear that the last one, just finished yesterday, has her orders for Limerick in Ireland. They say we are for Dublin but it is not settled. We got in here yesterday and will be loaded by Thursday most likely.

I was glad to see that your parrot was in good form. You did not say if you had taught it to whistle yet. I call the dog Nellie and she follows me everywhere. When I sometimes go in the Galley, she makes the Steward wild by rooting in the firegrate for ashes, scattering them all over the floor. But she only goes in when I do. I have not not found anybody to give her away to yet. Steward has got his baby's portrait enlarged and I have one of them for you.

Mrs. O'Neill had a 'cold pie' on deck this morning. They were in a hurry to catch the half past seven boat across to Seattle to go to early Mass. There was some frost on deck and in going to the boat she fell. When they got to the ferry, the steamer had just started, so they had to go right across on our own boat. Then it came on to snow very hard before they got back. They only came on board from the hospital on Wednesday and the Captain is none too well yet. So I hope he will not have got cold today, for it has been snow, rain and hail all day. So I have not been able to get to church today.

I see that Miss Martindale's half-brother, Captain Dawson, just arrived in Victoria a week ago, after being 192 days. They left Liverpool 2 days before us and the report says that the Mate and one man died of scurvy and others were sick. Mrs. Martindale would be very frightened, when he was not arriving, that the ship was lost; but another one of the same company's vessels is not arrived yet, after leaving Liverpool the same day.

The Steward's boy is still in the Hospital yet and is getting well very slowly; he may not be able to get back with us from here. We will all be very glad to get out of this cold country, though the days are beginning to get longer now very fast and the sun warmer, when it gets out. We had a very hard job to heave up our anchor

24

yesterday, though we had ten men to help us. It was down in 50 fathoms of water and not a half mile from the land. The chain would be equal to twice that, so we had a big weight to lift up.

This is Wednesday and we are nearly loaded. On Monday we had a very violent snow storm, almost a regular blizzard. It drove the snow into every crevice and nearly starved us all. The only warm place was the galley and it was freezing hard all the time. It has been frosty ever since; every place all around is covered with snow and ice.

We are coming to Queenstown for orders this time again and I hope to be home in the middle or latter part of June. We will finish loading tomorrow and sail on Saturday likely. Just got Uncle John's letter and paper yesterday and he thinks you are all learning to play music fast. I have not heard who is your teacher.

Friday 23rd February 92.
Finished loading and will leave here tomorrow morning early. In a few months I hope to be with you again and to find you very well. I see you never mention your Aunt H. Menhams; is she at home or at service again?

With best love to you, I conclude, Your Father,
T. Messenger.
Here is a little book for you and Aunt Hannah to read.

Queenstown.   *1892.*

My Dear Daughter,
I am glad to let you know that I am safe home in Port again and we have had a very nice and fairly good passage home, just 100 days. You will be beginning to look for me now.

I have just got your letter and I see you are quite well. I did have some eggs on Good Friday or Easter Sunday but not dyed, only fried for breakfast. What Aunt Ellen's baby is it that is nearly walking, where do they live?

The Captain's wife is very glad to be in Port again and I do not know whether she can stop to go to the final Port with the ship or not. We are all very well on board, only the Carpenter had a dip

Another picture of the crew of the Dunboyne

over the side this morning and got very much fagged out before we got him on board again. I should have written earlier today and got the letter sent away. Now it must wait until tomorrow. At any rate you would not have got it before Monday.

I think I must write to the Schoolmaster to see that you pay attention to your writing, as you do not improve very much at it. Or is it Jane Ann looks after you?

We will likely be here for a week or ten days, so you will have time to write again. Tell Aunt Lizzie I will write to them on Sunday when I have more time and let her know how much of my towel wants washing.

With kind love to you and Aunt Jane, also the rest at Birkby Moor. I am your loving Father,   *T. Messenger.*

LONDON TO VANCOUVER 1893

To My Dear Daughter,

I think to try to write you a little from time to time to record events. I thought to have had time to have sent you another letter by the Pilot but we did not have a Channel pilot on board.

Well, we got away from dock all right on Sunday morning at 7 o'clock and most of the crew were drunk but as we towed to Beachy head they had lots of time to get sobered up before we made sail. The steamer left us on Monday morning at 7 a.m., having towed us almost 150 miles. It was calm nearly all day but we got a nice fair wind at night which freshened nicely all day Tuesday and last night and today we have come along in fine style clear out of Channel, for which we are very grateful. It makes such a difference to beating about in the Channel for a week or so as we had to do before.

The baby is very ill and this afternoon they thought she would die but she has rallied a bit and Mrs O'Neill is in a sad state about her. The Captain is doctoring the child up and I hope she will recover though I have been very much afraid of it ever since we left. My little dog is all right, it does not get sea sick. The little wretch will bark and snap when I want it to keep quiet. Stewards leg is not yet better and the lad he has brought with him is a very awkward youth, which makes it worse for him.

Friday 11th August, evening, 7 p.m.
Have had a strong gale of wind from the S.W. ward yesterday and this morning but now it is moderate and fine. Poor little baby is not getting much better and we can only hope she will improve shortly. Steward keeps on growling at his lad. The youth can not learn to lay the table at all. He invariably sets us spoons for forks or vice versa, but he will learn in time no doubt.

The wind is keeping ahead very much but as yet we have no cause to grumble. At 4 o'clock today we passed a small Barque as if she were at anchor. I could read her name, the Rose of Devon, of Plymouth. Our ship seems to sail very well; this time at least we pass everything we come across yet. The puppy continues to thrive and our new boy is better of his sea sickness and is giving us Jack Robinson on his fiddle, while George Duff does the singing and keeping time. Mrs O'N. has to do her own washing for baby and Cpt. has to do the drying business.

Sunday 13th.
Buried the baby this evening at 8 o'clock. First we put the coffin over but it floated so we had to put more chain on it, or rather round it. Mrs. O'Neill is taking on very badly about it and so is the Captain. She died at noon yesterday, her little face and hands looked like wax as she lay in her coffin. Usually at sea we just bury people wrapped in canvas but Carpenter made a box and put the childs' name on it, just a fancy to please Mrs O'Neill. They put a diamond ring in the coffin, which was given to her by Mrs Thompson, the lady we picked up last passage. It is very fine, with a gentle southerly breeze and we are going along about 3 miles an hour in the right direction. I hope this death will be the only sad occurrence we will have to record this voyage. We could not find a church service on board; any amount of bibles but no prayer books. Even the mission box had not one in. It is just 12 months today since we left Barry Dock.

Thursday 17th. 7 o'clock in the evening.
We are still struggling on against a head wind, but the weather keeps very fine and I suppose the wind will change some day. Our crew are just about getting used to the ship now, getting in the way of things. And Steward's assistant, the lad, is more steady on his feet and manages to set the table out without forgetting quite so many things. Though he still says Captain instead of Sir when he speaks to the Cpt. He says "Will you have more tea Captain?" Sounds just a little too familiar you know for on board ship. Mrs O'Neill is getting over her grief for her baby now a little. A Norwegian Barque passed us on Sunday evening just as we lay hove to with our flag half mast ready to bury the child. We hoisted our numbers or letters (K.R.D.P.) so that she could report us when she

got home. Certain flags represent those letters and they in turn mean Dunboyne of Dublin and are called signal letters. I think everyone on board now is in good health, new boy included and as it is fine weather, we have plenty of work going on, so Goodnight.

Sunday Night 8 o'clock.
Just a week today since we buried poor little baby and a very fine week it has been. Today has been a most lovely day and we have two vessels in company. One close to us signalled she is a German from Freidrikstad for Adelaide with lumber, that is wood planks etc. she is 14 days out, we are 14. I think of you in your home and wonder what you are doing tonight and if the parrots are all well or not.

Monday 21st August.
The German ship yesterday is alongside, or was alongside this morning and it is the Anna Romein. We are passing her, leaving her behind a lot. She was in Rouen with us and at Wallaroo last January, so she is a kind of old companion. We have been busy taking down our good sails and putting up another set as we now are approaching the Trade wind region and may run right into them with the fine little fair wind we have. In fact it looks very much like it and the weather is a vast deal warmer. My little dog is getting very thin, I think it is sick. It lays in any coil of rope and watches the cat and wants to play with it. But pussy scratches too much for the dog. I may tell you that the Trade winds blow in the North Atlantic from the N.E. and in the South from the S.E. in the tropics and beyond, sometimes all the year round and it is mostly fine weather in them.

Wednesday 23rd.
Just about 100 miles off Madeira today and we have a good many vessels in company. We have a little fair wind yet and hope it will freshen into the North East Trades. We have plenty of work going on with now, repairing sails and ropes to get everything good when we get to Cape Horn. I have a clock in my room that I bought in London for 3 shillings and six pence but it ticks far too loud for me. The first night, I wound up the alarm by mistake and it went off

just as I was getting up at 12 0'clock (midnight). Stewards leg is nearly better now and his boy is not quite so awkward. The Carpenter is trying to frighten the fresh boys by telling them that he is preparing a razor to shave them with when we cross the Equator or else treat the sailors to a bottle of rum that was chiefly the passengers who had to pay. So they still go through a sort of shaving custom yet for fun.

Sunday 27th.

Very fine weather with a gentle breeze all the time and the sun is very hot, so hot we can not stand on deck barefooted. We are going on our way slowly and are going to make a long passage to the Line (Equator). Our youngest lad is a great fiddler so he keeps the boys amused in the dogwatch with his violin. The Carpenter also sings a good song, so we have a little concert usually each evening from 7 to 8 on deck, front of the Poop. It is always stopped at 8 o'clock because the watch below goes to bed then and comes out at midnight again. Steward's leg is about all right now; it takes him all his time giving his boy instructions, which he forgets as soon as out of hearing.

Hoping and trusting you are quite well, I am your father, Tom.

Thursday Night 8pm.

We have had a very nice breeze this week and lovely weather. The Carpenter is just singing along outside the boys' door here. A couple of mornings ago the ship was tossing some water on deck and threw some over the Boatswain (Bosun) as he was sleeping on the carpenters' bench outside his room door. He said the bugs had driven him out and then the sea drove him in at 5 o'clock in the morning, just as we were getting coffee and everybody laughed very much. The little dog was nearly killed this morning; it was round the carpentery bench and a lump off a plank fell on it. Someone said it never said anything at first but walked round the house and as soon as it saw someone, it set up a terrible howl and everyone thought its leg was broken and Bosun had splints and bandages ready for use. However after a little coaxing and patting, she got upon her legs and trotted away, not much worse.

Sunday Sept 3rd 1893. Evening 8pm.

It has been nearly calm all day today and very hot. Just after noon, a shark came round the ship and Boatswain put the hook over with a piece of pork on it and the shark took it at once. There was a rush to get it on board, which was done at last after a fierce struggle for freedom on the shark's part. It took all hands to pull it over the rail. I had it measured on deck and it was just ten feet long. The backbone and jawbone was soon cut out. The tail was chopped off first thing to keep it quiet. There was another big one alongside and a lot of Pilot fish; they always accompany big sharks about. We did not get any of them or the other shark. But we have got a little breeze starting up which we like much better. The Trades are starting up afresh again and we hope they will carry us along a good bit farther yet, as we are still 900 miles from the Equator, 28 days out from London now. So good night, I am going to bed.

Monday 4th.

Had and still have a 5 knot breeze all night. The ship Gifford still keeps about a mile astern. He got nearly up to us yesterday but has dropped a bit again. Mrs O'Neill was playing the piano a bit today, about the first time since we left. She feels the hot weather very much and so does the little pup. I call her Nell but she does not seem to take kindly to the name yet. I had to do a small wash today, my shirt and unmentionables and I am not proud of my handiwork.

Wednesday 6th.

What a night we had last night for rain and squalls and black as could be till 2 o'clock this morning when the moon got up and it was much lighter and the rain stopped. but it came down worse than ever at 4 o'clock and our Main Top Sail got burst, so we had to shift it at daylight. The wind was right ahead all night but it has got up fine weather today and this evening we signalled the ship Duke of Edinburgh, from Calcutta to London, 89 days out. The Carpenter got all his clothes wet in his chest this morning. He lifted it out of the house to dry the place up and she took a very unexpected sea on deck and washed his chest away, wetting the things. She also filled the house and drenched the boys thoroughly. Of course as it is hot weather, they had not much clothes on. I had to run for my life to get clear of it.

Friday 8th.
Plenty of rain these last two days and nights. I did a considerable amount of washing yesterday, my clothes and blankets, so I am waiting for a chance to get them dry. I don't think I made a good job of the blankets but it will freshen them at any rate. There are clothes hanging about the ship in all directions as everybody takes the chance of plenty of fresh water to wash up their clothes. Mostly all sailors bring their clothes on board dirty unless they are young men from their own homes. As we are nearing the Equator, they are trying to scare the hands (men) that have not crossed the Line before, telling them how they will shave them. The dog has just learned to go up the ladder on the Poop. It has got very thin. It is very dark and looks like plenty of rain again tonight; I hope it won't though.

Sunday 10th.
I think we will cross the line about the same date this year as we did last. That is making a longer passage of it by 5 days. It has been very pleasant today, fine and dry. I got all my clothes dry yesterday and it will be 3 weeks before I wash my blankets, before we get into wild weather again. You will most likely be in chapel or church now as it is 7 o'clock.

Thursday Sept. 14th.
Here we are still nearly 100 miles off the line, yet the wind remains right ahead, so that we are making little progress in the right way. However it shows signs of veering to the S.E. now, so we will probably get across tomorrow night if we keep going ahead as we are at present. It is keeping lovely fine weather for us now so we are jogging along, enjoying life in a quiet fashion. Watch in, watch out, the days pass by slowly and surely and this will be our longest passage out to the Equator. I have been sewing a bit today, at a new sail and have skinned my finger and thumb, not being used to working so hard.

Saturday 16th.

Well we crossed the Equator yesterday, so last night all those who had not crossed the Line before were shaved according to the old custom. Father Neptune in the person of the Carpenter came on board and asked for all the new hands. He wore a long white beard made of white rope yarns and with him he had two policeman to help him and the Steward was the barber. They were placed on a bench and well lathered with some nasty mixture, then shaved with a big wooden razor. Then they were given a pill or two and a mixture of salts and lime juice : the elixir of life. Then they plumped them overhead in a tub full of water. Mrs O'Neill said it was too bad, but a glass of rum set them all right again. The Dublin boy has cleaned the razor and rolled it up in paper to take home to his Ma to let her see what he was shaved with.

Monday 18th.

Yesterday we had a Barque in company but she ran clean away from us and was clear out of sight this morning; the worst beating we have had for this passage. I see there are a lot of barnacles, that is a kind of shellfish, growing all along the side of the ship and if they are as bad on the bottom, they will stop the ship a good deal. They are all in front of the cabin here, talking about London and the boy is fiddling for them but no-one sings tonight. The little dog is growing fast and is a great pet. Gets its feed from anybody and everybody and plays around with the cat. The Carpenter last week made a very nice dressing table to go in the corner of the bathroom and it looks very nice. The old Bosun makes sails now.

Sunday 24th.

Very fine weather we have had this week, calms and light airs. Today we have a nice wind but the ship keeps rolling from side to side in a very uncomfortable manner. We caught a large moth or butterfly yesterday and a very pretty one it is. It must have been blown off the Brazilian coast about 300 miles or more. We are getting down South slowly and may soon look out for squalls ahead. It was threatening yesterday but the wind today has cleared the sky. Tonight it is a little more gloomy ahead and we may expect a change before long and then our work and trouble begins until we get round Cape Horn. A large four-mast American schooner passed away across our bows to the SSE, likely bound East to China or Japan, as a great many go out that way with paraffin oil in cases.

I wonder how you are all getting on at home tonight it will soon be getting Winter time. I hope the parrots are all right.

Tuesday Night 26th.
Our fine breeze on Sunday finished up at midnight and from 1 0'clock till 6 o'clock it rained solid as hard as it could and we had to snug down to it. It kept only a light wind all day yesterday but last night and today, we had a strong gale from the SW right ahead for us and fine dry weather with it. Now it has dropped away to a calm almost. The Carpenter had his hand cut by the boy at the dinner table today; the boy clumsily ran the table knife into it. It has been quite cold today, so that I could not get warm in my bunk this morning at all.

Wednesday 27th. Latitude 22 45S.
Saw two Cape pigeons today. They are very rarely seen so far North but the South wind has likely brought them up.

Saturday 30th.
We are nearly two months at sea now and are getting on very slowly. Here we are not much beyond the Tropics and cold enough to be 40 South. Will just have to get out all my warmer clothes now. That new bed tick Aunt Lizzie made is very cold to lie on now. I do not know what it will be when we get off Cape Horn. The ship was giving us a little taste of what we are to expect bye and bye, tossing water on board right in the cabin door.

Wednesday October 4th 1893.
We have been making a little more progress these last few days; had quite a gale last night. Heard her slapping water over the decks and she jumped into the head sea pretty considerable. We gave our signal letters R.R.A.P. to two steamers on Monday and Tuesday and they will likely report us in about a month's time. We were down below, re-securing the cargo in the after hold and found someone had been stealing beer from the cases aft. Three loose

bottles were found away at the other end of the ship. Just shows
what sailors will do for beer. I have had to do some mending at my
jacket and trousers and made a very creditable job of the patches.
There is a little Barque in company today but we are passing him
fast and will be too far off to see who it is in the morning. My dog
Nelly and the cat are great friends, except when they quarrel over
their food. Then Nelly is cross; she is more gluttonous than the cat.
There is George Duff singing Maggie Murphy's Home.

Thursday 5th.
Very light breeze and pleasant clear weather this morning and
forenoon. We passed no fewer than 5 Pilot schooners belonging to
Buenos Aires. Two of them came close to and asked us where we
were bound. They are over two hundred miles out from Buenos
Aires and 120 from land, so we were very much surprised to see
them. A very large school of porpoises passed the ship today; the
water was fairly boiling with them as far as we could see. They were
jumping and tumbling in a most playful, lively manner. We also
passed some seals playing and popping their comical little dog's
heads up every now and then to take a look at us going past them.
A very lovely day indeed has today been.

   We are like you at home now, getting colder weather every day.
But we are going to the cold weather and it is coming to you in
England. We are lengthening our days while yours are growing
shorter. By the time we reach Cape Horn, we will have light until
8 o'clock and at 4 in the morning. It is now 7 and 5 light.

Friday 6th.
A dull foggy day and worse, for the wind went ahead this afternoon much to our disgust and it is now very cold. Have had to get
a fire in the cabin to keep the Mrs. warm.

Sunday 8th.
After two days beating to windward with a strong SSW wind, we
are just back where we started from and it is very cold on deck. The
wind blows through you so. A big 4-master has been in company
with us these two days but has done no better than us. I have just
had to mend my old overcoat to put on at 8 o'clock when I go on

deck, good Sabbath night as it is. Mrs O'Neill on the Poop this evening thought she was like to be blown up, the wind got round her legs so. All our warm clothing has had to be brought out for this cold icy wind but when it shifts, we will have it warm again.
Lat. 37 0S. Long 54 1/2W.

Tuesday Evening.
We have had a nice little fair wind at last for just 16 hours and now it is nearly a calm. It is raining hard with the glass falling, so I hear the Captain on deck is getting the sails off the ship, though I think we will not have much wind. At any rate, it is many degrees warmer today; even the little dog feels that. When it is cold she likes to sneak into the saloon beside Mrs. O'Neill and the stove, but she soon drops her tail and hangs her head when the boy comes in.

I am wondering if your parrots keep alive still and if you are getting tired of them already. How the rain is falling. I wonder if I am going to have a wet watch until 12 tonight. I think not, it is only a passing shower.

The shower wound up in a hard gale before 12. Had to call all hands out to shorten sail. It came on so very fast and the sea all around was lit up by phosphoric light. It looked like vast numbers of electric lights darting here and there as the seas curled and crested. It blew hard until sunrise, then moderated.

Saturday Evening.
Very fine weather again, these last two days and we have managed to get a little farther along on our journey. The weather is much warmer, with the wind from the North and we may get on quietly down to Staten Land. As this is Saturday night and fine, I have had a general wash and change. You see we have to take advantage of a fine warm day to get a decent wash now down here and more so when we get a bit farther South into colder weather. We are 70 days from London tomorrow and are likely to be another 14 or more to Cape Horn.

Friday Afternoon, 4 o'clock.
Here we are, right off the entrance to the Straits of Lemaire, the

passage between Staten Land and Tierra del Fuego. It is about 10 mile wide and the same through, but the Captain will not run into it as the tide is against us after 8 o'clock. So we are going away round Staten Land, 40 miles back again and that is a consideration. Means losing at least 20 miles distance. We are glad to have a good breeze in our favour at any rate and we are having fine warm weather for this place but the snow on the land looks cold. We had it very thick and one day foggy for the last few days. The little dog will get into the bunk to sleep and I put her out. She goes into the 2nd Mate's room, into the 3rd Mate's bunk and it is easy to get in there. I had a very bad ear ache all last night and Mrs O'Neill gave me some Chloric Ether to put in it but I can't say it has done any good. It is better now when I am below.

Sunday October 22nd 1893.
Here we have got at last just a degree (60 miles) South of the Diego Ramirez, some islands South and West of South America. We are stuck with a gale from the West dead against us; when the squalls come down on us it is very cold, but yet not more so than we had it in 37 South a fortnight ago. I see that we have got down around Cape Horn quicker than I expected and if we could only get a southerly wind now, we could do some good with it. My ear ache and neuralgia left me as sudden as they came. I turned out and they were there; I turned out again and they were gone. Now I want to get into some warmer weather. I am like the little dog here; I dislike cold weather very much, chiefly because I feel so cold in bed. I do not mind it so much while I am on deck. Nelly will hardly eat anything at all; she is sick and got very thin. She only eats preserved meat at any time and fancy biscuits the Mrs. gives her.

I trust you are quite well at home tonight and wondering where your father is at times; I dare say so. Goodnight.

Tuesday 24th.
Just 60 miles farther back today than we were 2 days ago, as it has been a hard gale from SW and West. So we were not much surprised to see the Island of Cape Horn today. Just at 4 o'clock this afternoon, she shipped a dollop of water in amidships and knocked the new boy on his back. He got up very pale and gasped for breath

but when he saw Mrs O'Neill on the Poop laughing at him, he pulled up a brave face again. I got my boots full watching him. Have had to do some needle work on a pair of trousers this evening, or else wear my best ones, so I put a nice square patch on the knee that would pass examination at school. I hope we may get a fair wind soon and get into warm weather.

Thursday 26th.
Here we have been all day, tumbling about in a terrible disagreeable fashion. Yesterday afternoon, we got a nice fair wind and the sea fell, so we got all sails set for a few hours and managed to get a couple of degrees, 70 miles or so, to the Westward; but from 10 to 12 last night, they had all their work cut out getting sail off the ship in time. Fortunately, the sea was smooth. This morning from 4 to 6, it blew a fair howling gale and set up a terrible sea that set the ship kicking up in fine style. We had to be careful how we held things at the table and I wonder how the Steward managed to get anything cooked at all. It is a bit finer and the ship is a good deal easier now. We have got some more canvas on her but the wind is ahead. Put the little dog out on deck this morning and she got washed across the deck from side to side and she made tracks for my bunk as soon as she got inside again. I had to take her on the Poop deck to dry and shut my room door. This weather is bad for her, she misbehaves herself so. Mrs O'Neill feeds her on plum duff, Thursdays and Sundays. The Steward's lad is doing very well this bad weather, getting around much better than I expected.

Another Sunday has come and gone and we have had a few hours pleasant sunshine after a week tumbling about. Last night was quite a miserable one, with hail squalls and the ship tumbling about all ways, so it was quite a relief when I was able to set all sails this morning. Though this afternoon we had to take them in again, as it is coming on to blow from ahead again. I wish we were out of this cold stormy weather, I have had enough of it for a time now. It is too cold to sit still to read, when the ship will let us do so. The poor dog Nellie is about starved to death and does like to get into my berth on top of the rug. I have to shut her out though, or my things would smell too much of doggie. Two of the lads are laid up, one with a sore throat and the young one got his foot sprained yesterday, being knocked up by a sea. He is no loss anyway, being simply useless this weather.

I look at your likenesses and wish your mother was alive yet; but you will scarcely remember her.

Monday 29th.
Well we had a very hard gale last night, up until daylight this morning, when we got a fair wind from the SW and had to turn the ship round at 4am. While doing so she was nearly washing people away from the braces (ropes) but the wind did not last long, for it has died away to a calm. This evening we got all sails set again however and hope for a favourable wind again soon. The dog got a washing across the deck again this afternoon coming from the galley. Some water came on deck and sent her across to leeward. Then she ran back to the galley as hard as she could and lay down in front of the stove to dry. Seem not to be feeling the cold near so much lately myself, at least since I thought on to put my big rug Aunt Jane bought me on top of my bed; and doesn't the dog like to lay on it to sleep. She only goes to the galley when the Steward has something for her to eat; fresh meat.

Wednesday Nov. 1st 1893.
Now we are on our way rejoicing, with a fine fair wind, or rather what sailors call a Yankee start, that is very nearly fair. As the ship is jogging along at 8 or 9 knots, we are a little exultant over it and we are already anticipating warmer weather. However we must not 'Hallo' till we are out of the wood, as our breeze may not last us very long.

A large ship passed us early this morning which had lost her main Top mast; we could not see which ship it was.

I look at my rug and think of your Aunt; I seem hardly to realise that she is gone and our home broken up. Well she is at rest and happy, I have no doubt.

Friday 3rd.
Have had two gales of wind since I last wrote. Our fair wind finished with a hard gale from the SW for a few hours, then calmed and the wind shifted to the NW last night. Then we had another

gale, with plenty of rain until daylight this morning, when it came back favourable again. It has been so all day, giving us another little chance to get North into warmer weather again. I think we feel it warmer already. We had one of our sails blown into ribbons last evening in a squall, trying to pull it down - the outer Jib, forward sail of all.

Sunday Nov. 5th 1893.

This has been a very fine day, only a gloomy one, the sun never having shewn out at all; but we have a nice breeze carrying us to the North, into warmer weather. A Barque passed close-to this fore-noon; we signalled her and it was the Doon of Ayr, 817 tons, from Lobos Island for Cork, 24 days out. They only get guano from that place and it is away up North of Peru near to the Equator. We are getting into milder weather and I am very glad of it. Cold weather I detest at sea and I think the little dog will be glad of it. She has grown a big dog now but not as big as her mother yet.

Monday 6th.

Same light breeze and a gloomy day, very fine weather. We have had two Barques in company. We signalled one, the Penrhyn Castle from Buenos Aires for Conception Bay, 36 days out; 4 days more than we have been since seeing the Pilot schooners of the river there. The other Barque must be going to the same place. They have only 500 miles to go now. Both are in ballast.

Sunday 12th.

There is nearly a week passed since I wrote anything and, during that time, we have managed to crawl slowly up with warmer weather and dispensed with the cabin fire. At present we are having lovely weather, fine and clear and are just passing the Island of Masapuera. We saw it at daylight, 5.30 this morning and have been sailing towards it at 6 or 7 knots and are only abreast now, 5 o'clock this evening. So have seen it nearly 80 miles away. We are all glad to find ourselves in warm weather once again, even the dog and cat also. Now our Spring cleaning commences, from the masthead to the water!

Now I hope you are all well at home and that you have not

neglected your parrots. Your Aunt will likely be at home and teach them to whistle.

Wednesday 15th.
Well we have got into the SE Trades now and are rolling along slowly in anything but an easy manner, making 130 to 140 miles a day. All hands are busy tarring down the rigging and two pots of tar were spilt on deck today; one dropped the pot altogether. It is not so easy holding on with the ship rolling so. We are getting into nice warm weather now and should reach the Equator in another 14 days or so. So we may get out inside of 150 days yet. I think there is no-one better pleased to get into warmer weather than the dog; the cat and it are great play-mates. I have to get all my warm, heavy clothing put away for a month or so now.

Sunday 19th.
Here we are, sailing along quietly and peacefully up the South Pacific ocean and nothing in sight but a few Mother Carey's chickens (that is stormy petrels). The weather is just cold enough at night time to require blankets yet, though we are well inside the Tropics now. As this is Sunday, there were a few clothes hanging out to dry, or rather air. Mrs O'Neill said that the moths had been at her best jacket and at a muff, in spite of stuff she put in to keep them out. They have been contented with eating my mufflettes and socks, though perhaps some carbolic soap I have keeps them out of my bedclothes. I feel the sun has been at my ears, they are burning very much and my nose is just recovering from a little break-out. I am very afraid I will be left with a very red carbuncle nose, if it keeps on breaking out much more; and I will be like poor old Will Reay, the Carpenter.

Our days are gradually getting shorter, it is dark at 7 and not light until after 5. So we will have no more long days until we get to the North Atlantic on our way home again. The boy is just playing the Cottage by the Sea on the fiddle; the Mrs never tunes the piano at all now.

Thursday 23rd.
We are making a little more progress these last few days, just

getting into regular Trade wind weather, a brisk breeze and showery. We have just got the ship all scrubbed and ready for painting
and we ought to cross the Line in a weeks' time. The weather keeps
chilly at nights and I find my blankets necessary yet. Our chickens
have lived round Cape Horn but do not lay any eggs now. So the
Steward killed the rooster today and stewed it, so we can still have
a fresh mess in spite of nearly 4 months at sea.

Monday Nov 27th.
Still sailing on slowly in a dreamy kind of way, the weather being
beautifully soft and clear, Latitude 6 South today, 113 days out.
Will likely be about 8 weeks more yet. yesterday, Boatswain caught
a rat and neither dog nor cat would tackle it, they would only sniff
at it. Today he caught two more. The dog, after playing with the rat
yesterday, went into a fit and has not been well since.

Friday Dec 1st.
Will cross the Equator about midnight tonight, thus making 117
days from London. We have had a strong S. Westerly current
against us these last few days, which has kept us back over a degree.
The Boatswain keeps on catching rats, about seven in all. Last night,
I had a try after one in my room. It woke me up running over me,
so I got up after it at half past eleven and chased it round the chest
and desk but it got away. I think it must have come in through the
Port; the dog was not in the room at the time, or between us we
might have got it.

The Carpenter has been cutting the saloon table and they have
shifted the piano from the after cabin into the saloon. The Mrs.
never plays any though. We have got the ship all nicely painted
round now and she looks very well indeed. I hope we may have a
fine passage up from here now and keep her clean. I am beginning
to weary of it and long for a letter from you to tell me how you and
Aunt and Grandma and the kids all are. My dog is sick yet, does not
seem to be able to find an easy place for herself.

Thursday 7th.
We have at last got well across the Equator into 7 degrees North and
have landed into a calm, the sun scorching all day. We have nearly

finished all our painting and are doing a little cleaning over the side now. There is always plenty of work in an iron ship, knocking paint off and putting on fresh, if we have the paint. Last evening, we got two sharks, so the boys are cleaning their backbones for walking sticks. This evening, the Captain shot one as it swam after the ship. When he hit it, it flung itself half out of the water. The other evening, lots of fishes were playing, some throwing themselves 20ft in the air. A number of bosuns (a bird with a long feather in their tails like a marlinspike, from which they get their name, boatswain's on board ship having charge of such things.) We only made 20 miles in the last 24 hours and are not going to do much more the next, so we are not going to get to Port for Christmas.

Saturday Evening 9th.
We did not have a calm for long. Got a nice breeze at dark the other night and it has settled into good NE Trade winds, so we are going on our way rejoicing. 126 days out tomorrow. We got our decks oiled yesterday and she commenced to wash water across them. We can hardly stand on them now; one fellow got a nice tumble this evening.

Friday 15th.
We are making very good progress and hope to get in by the New Year yet, all well. Got some damage done to our sails last night; burst two of them and had a job getting another one aloft, being a strong wind and squally at the time (midnight). It has been blowing fresh all day today and the ship tumbling about a bit but we don't mind that so much, so long as we are going on our way cheerily.

Now we have to bring out our blankets and top-coats again. A great deal of washing was done in the rain yesterday but there is too much sea on to do any drying today. I am just going to do a little wash myself now, my dirty flannels from Cape Horn. I have just had to remove the dog from the room out of my way.

Tuesday 19th Dec.
Dear Mary, we are surely and gradually drawing nearer to journey's end and a few days of favourable wind should put us into our desired Port. We continue to have fine and pleasant

weather and yesterday we had a ship in sight going North like ourselves, the first one we have seen for six weeks. Today, a Barque passed going South. The weather is quite cold at nights and all my warm clothes are being brought out into use again. The days are also getting short with us; it is dark soon after 5 and not daylight until after half past 6. The Captain has been making alterations in the After cabins, cut the saloon table and put the piano outside, making the After cabin just as it was at first. Mrs O'Neill has been putting gold paint on the canary cage today and it does shine up, looks brighter than gold leaf.

Thursday Dec. 21st.
Still keep going on our way rejoicing, with a favourable wind but the ship has been tumbling about a good deal yesterday and today. Mrs. O'Neill's gold paint changed colour and as we laughed at it she has painted it over yellow, before she puts the gold on again; she says it was the red shining through it before that made it change colour so.

We are just 600 miles from the entrance to the Straits at Vancouver and hope to get up there the beginning of next week.

Saturday 23rd.
Well we have had two days uneasy time of it, the ship filling the decks with water and today we have had plenty of rain. I have had to lock the drawers under my bed, as she was sliding them out every heavy roll she made. We are just about thoroughly sick and tired of perpetual rolling, although we are going the right way all the time. In fact the wind is too fair; it is right behind us. We would prefer it at the side to keep her steady.

Steward says the boys are all wanting to know what they are going to get for Christmas. Soft bread and plum pudding; we will not have any roast beef. The dog has just come into the room looking very miserable and wet and as much as says "Let me stop here, it isn't fit for a dog outside!" So I put her up on the sofa with my jacket for a bed and she is off to sleep. More than what I can do though; I fit myself up like the dog, to keep myself from rolling.

Monday Dec. 25th.

This is Christmas Day and here we are in a calm, tumbling about with the sea in all ways and we are only 90 miles off Cape Flattery and about 130 from there up to Vancouver City. When we get up the Straits, we expect to get a tug to tow us up there. The weather is getting rather chilly, though not very cold as yet.

Of course I have been thinking much of you at home today and wondering if you are having a fine Christmas. Perhaps you are writing me a letter, if you have not already written. I hope your parrots keep well. I hear there is a seal around the ship, as it is barking like a dog now and again, as it pops its head out of the water. We saw them firing a gun on board a Schooner that passed at 4 o'clock; perhaps they were firing at it then. I think everyone has been stuffed out with plum pudding and mince pies today and I hear of no-one being a bit ill. Only the dog is ill, or sleepy and can't tell which.

Wednesday 27th.

At last we are up to Cape Flattery, after beating to windward yesterday and today, all day. We are just at the entrance to the Straits, a very light East wind dead against us. They signalled from the shore they would send a tug, so we may get a steamer in the morning. It is 60 miles from here to Victoria and as much more from there to Vancouver. The high hills are all covered with snow and it blows very cold off them. Mrs.O'Neill says she has not been so cold for a long time; no more have I.

SEATTLE TO U.K., 1894.

Ship Dunboyne, Seattle   *January 17th, 1894.*

My Dear Daughter,
I received your letter and was very much shocked at the news of
your Aunt Ann's death. In fact I could hardly believe it true and
read again and again to see if I was not mistaken. I have got a letter
from Mary Lizzie also and I can imagine how they will all miss her
in their home; but time will make them do so. She just mentioned
in her letter to me two very sudden deaths in Carlisle and how it did
behove one to be prepared for a sudden call. How very little I
suppose she thought she would be the one to go without a moment's warning. But so it is and 'one shall be taken and the other
left'.

We got here yesterday forenoon, after being 48 hours getting
here. We just got within 5 miles the other afternoon, when it came
down a perfect hurricane for a little while and the steamboat could
not hold us. So we set some sails and run back to anchor for the
night. We have had some very wild wet weather here, blowing a
gale all the time nearly. We are going to put all cargo out here and
load here also; not going to Tacoma at all and I am very glad of it.
This is a much better place, quite a fine city, much bigger than
Vancouver. The tramways, or streetcars as they call them here, are
all over the town and well out in the country. Electric cars, cable
cars and steam cars; they nearly take in every street and go very
fast, far faster than the London trams.

We don't expect to be here more than 3 weeks now, as they will
soon put the wheat in at the elevator. They simply pour it in as fast
as we can stow it away. I shall be glad when we do get away into
warmer weather; I am tired of this cold, really don't like it.

I thought I had lost my little dog last night. I did lose her on the
street, but this forenoon she came back on board; found her way
back and was glad to get back. It is raining now and I hear her
outside the cabin, whining to get in. She won't go to the galley to the

47

watchman.

There is a great number of people here out of work. Everything is very dull and quiet and only that the town is keeping a great number employed or it would be worse. They say that the Salvation Army are feeding about 300 people, giving them a meal a day. All the same, saloon and theatres do a good business. Men, women and children may starve, but the people must be entertained at all costs.

Who is teaching you music, you do not say. Will you be able to play a tune on the piano for me when I come home; about June I hope to.

With kind love from your Father,   *T. Messenger.*
Hoping Aunt H., Grandfather and Mother are quite well.

Ship Dunboyne, Seattle, Washington.   *February 4th 1894.*

My Dear Daughter,
I received your letter all right and was glad to see you were quite well and also Grandfather and Mother.

We have a good many sick people on board here at present. The Captain is very ill and has been for 10 days. The Steward is bad and his boy I took to the Hospital yesterday. Some of the men are also more or less ill. In fact I myself am about the best on board at present, although I do lie shivering half the night when it is very cold.

It has been steady rain nearly all day today, except a couple of hours this afternoon. Now it is just pouring down. I rather like it to rain because it is generally much warmer than when it is dry and frosty. I don't want all the clothes I can find to cover me until I am not able to move under them.

The Doctor wanted to send Captain O'Neill to Hospital today and Mrs. O'Neill with him, but she would not go. But if he is no better tomorrow, they will likely go. They have the finest hospital here I have ever seen, that is the most comfortable rooms, all attended by Sisters of Mercy. I just thought if I was living on shore here, I would like to go and live in the Hospital.

We had a lady and three children on board this afternoon, to see the Captain. She was a Captain's wife and, hearing of Captain

O'Neill's sickness, came to see him and sent him some jelly. But he is too sick to eat much. The dog fairly ran away from the children; she was frightened of them. It is the 'Gripki' or influenza that is making everybody sick; I hope I may keep clear of it.

We have got out in the Bay to anchor and wait our turn to get the remainder of our cargo and we are not likely to get any this week, so they say. So we will be here another fortnight yet, I fully expect. If we were only free of this influenza on board, I would not care; as we are laying very nice and quiet here clear of the shore and not spending much money, which is a consideration.

A good many of the crew have been getting their likenesses taken here. I did not bother about mine, as we will have them taken together when I get home again, if I should be spared to do so. I hope your Aunt Lizzie is altogether better now; perhaps nursing does not agree with her.

With kind love to yourself and Grandma and all, I remain
Your Loving Father,   *T. Messenger.*

(Captain and Mrs O'Neill are going to the Hospital this afternoon).

Ship Dunboyne, Columbia River.

My Dear Daughter,
As we are laying at anchor here for a day or two, unable to get out, I must just write you a few lines again.

We are just laying about half way between Astoria and the bar, which we dare not cross because there is too much sea on it and the ship might strike the ground. But I am in hopes that we shall not have to wait much longer, as the weather is considerably more settled now. I shall not be at home this year for your Band of Hope trip, wherever it may be to, but possibly I will be at home for some other trip; or we will have to make one of our own somewhere during your School holiday.

I am very pleased to say that I am keeping in the best possible health all the time and I hope that you and Aunt Jane are also keeping well during this hard Winter. How you must have enjoyed the frosty weather, sliding about. I remember how much I enjoyed

The Dunboyne, re-named AF Chapman, circa 1950

it myself when I was your age, sliding until my trousers used to freeze about me and getting up before daylight to water the slide. But I would rather be without the frost now; it is too hard for old people like me and the rest of your Uncles and Aunts, though we all fancy ourselves quite young yet.

I hope to get home to you sometime in June or early July and you will think that is a long while to look forward to. And so it is, but it will soon pass over, though I have a long way to come and a rough sea to travel over before we reach Hull. I wonder if you recollect anything about Hull, but I suppose you will not; only that from there you went to Sheffield for a day to see your

Mother's Aunt and now they are both dead.

With love to you and Aunt Jane and also all at the Moor, I remain your loving Father,   *T. Messenger*

Ship Dunboyne.   *May 27th, 1894.*

My Dear Daughter,

I wonder if you are quite well. It does seem such a long time since I last heard from you and yet we have been making very good time so far on our way home. We are now at the limits of the NE Trade winds, in 26 North and should easy be in Queenstown in less than 20 days. We are now out 90 days, which is very good work so far and if we get in by 110 days, we will have made a very good passage.

My little dog is very sick today. She looks up very piteously, clambering on my lap to pet her a bit; but she is in too much pain to rest anywhere. She has been in grand trim all this passage, running around and playing all the time. I think she must have been licking the paint off herself, as she got all over paint. Yesterday I had her in a tub of water and gave her a good wash; she has not been well since.

Of course we are very busy painting up the Dunboyne to make her shine when we get home. Most of the paint is on now, but we have the decks to 'holystone' down yet, the worst job of all. Everybody seems to make their minds up that the ship will go to Antwerp. There is an Exhibition on there this year and plenty of attractions to spend their money there. But I take it we will not go there just because everyone wants to.

We have had a wonderfully fine passage all the way so far and I hope we will carry our fine weather into Port with us. Mrs O'Neill is very anxious to get home, as she will soon have another baby to take the place of the one they lost.

Sunday June 10th.

Now we are nearing home steadily and hope to be in Queenstown by Thursday at the latest. We have kept coming on our way easily and steadily, always a little breeze and fine weather, with a wonderfully smooth sea all the time. Now we are so near, the time seems long. Mrs O'Neill thinks the days a terrible length and the ship very slow, though in reality she is fast past everything we come across.

We are all painted up and clean, ready for Port and hoping to be sent to Dublin or Antwerp. For myself, I care little where we go to.

We have a fine breeze now from the North that would take us in by Wednesday easy if it held. The little dog is all on the move and covered with all coloured paints. I tried her with a rat to see if she would tackle it. She ran around after it madly and pawed it about, but would not bite it. She is always looking below for rats to chase around.

I am wondering if you will be able to play me a tune by the time I get home and if you get on with your music well. Which of you learns fastest, you or Annie?

I am pleased to say I am in excellent health and have been all the voyage, bar feeling my leg tired sometimes. I shall be glad when we get into Port and I hear if you are all well at home.   So Goodnight.

Thursday Evening, June 14th, Off Cape Clear.
Now we are getting near journey's end; I can hear the guns firing at Fastnet rock 20 miles away. One fisherman told us at 4 o'clock we were 20 miles off. Another at 6 told us we were 10 or 11, so I suppose that we are about 15. From here to Queenstown is about 60 miles, so at our present rate, we ought to be in to anchor tomorrow in good time. It has been very foggy and very light air this last two days and disappointing not to get in today. We had some fresh fish for tea from the boatman, but they were fearfully salty.

I had quite a job to get my dog washed anyways decent today. She was so covered with paint and oil and Mrs O'Neill thought she ought to go into Port clean. I had a job to catch her, for as soon as she saw the preparations, she cleared out.

Now you must write back by return of post, as I know you will not get this before Monday and I will not get your answer before Wednesday; we will probably be leaving on Thursday. Trusting this finds you all well at Moor Park,
    I remain your Father,   *T.M.*

Friday 6 pm.
Just turning into harbour, after being outside in a fog all day. Now it is fine and clear and we will anchor in an hours time.

The AF Chapman (ex Dunboyne) May 1998. Permanently berthed in Stockholm harbour

MAIDEN VOYAGE OF THE LADAS
TOM MESSENGER'S
FIRST COMMAND
MARYPORT TO CORRAL, CHILE.

Barque Ladas,   *Wednesday, August 22nd, 1894.*

My Dear Daughter,
Now we are clear off to sea outside the Channel and everybody is about getting used to the ship. The boys are all free from sickness and the Carpenter also. We have not had any rolling about of any consequence; only on one day was the ship a little uneasy. She sails very well, leaving everything behind that we have come across yet, the Brierholme amongst the number we have passed. We passed her abreast of Dublin Bay on Sunday evening.

I am very pleased with my first command so far and am glad to have had such fine weather, though we are not doing much as yet towards making a smart passage. The wind is ahead most of the time but we hope to be favoured soon. It is raining very heavy just at present and I find it very nice when I can please myself if I go out amongst it or not. I have had to cut a hole in the side of my shoes to give easement to my feet, as they are very sore.

I quite failed to see where you had stowed yourself on the pier as we towed out; I could not see you anywhere. Mostly all our crew were more or less tipsy, so I had a job to get the sails set. I let the steamer go off St. Bees Head, getting abreast of Douglas that night at 9 o'clock and clear away out of the Channel 30 hours later, very glad of it.

Thursday 23rd
Calm most of this day and at 8 tonight it is raining very hard, with a faint fair NE wind; so perhaps we may be getting a bit of a run soon from it, as we will soon be out a week now and little progress.

The Barque Ladas. Built Maryport 1894. Named after the Derby winner

Saturday 25th August.
Very fine, warm and calm weather, just making about 30 miles a day. Two other vessels in company, sea very smooth. All the boys all right now, clear of sicknesss. The weather is warm and I have got off my stockings, though I have to put shoes on to go on deck, on account of so much pitch and tar about. One of the chickens died the other day and we killed one today for dinner tomorrow.

Sunday 26th.
Well we had the chicken for dinner; it was a very fine one and well cooked. The Cook and Steward are both very good and clean and I am glad of it.

  We are still getting nothing but head wind; very fine weather all the time, but making very little progress. I hope to get better luck soon, or the Ladas will get a bad name to start with.

Wednesday 29th.
We have been doing a little better this last 3 days; I do hope our breeze will keep on and carry us into the Trades. We are at least having lovely weather and sea smooth as oil. The ship is gliding along easy and peacefully. I seem quite to miss Mrs. O'Neill a lot. She was always so cheerful and chatty and having so much time to spare I feel sometimes a little lonely. I get to bed at midnight generally and sleep off and on until 8 in the morning. I generally do an hour's sleep afternoon 3 to 5 and, at frequent intervals, I grumble at the small distance we are making. We are having all the road to ourselves, no vessels in company.

Saturday September 1st, 1894.
We are 14 days out today and still 180 miles or so from the Island of Madeira, very slow progress so far. Yesterday and last night, we had any quantity of lightning and thunder, which gradually passed away by daybreak today. Now we have a nice pleasant fair wind and hope it will carry us into the Trades soon. Mr Ritson will likely flatter himself we are many miles further ahead than we are. The ship is doing her best and sails very fast when she gets the chance, but we can do nothing without wind.

Sunday 2nd.
We sighted the Island at 2 o'clock this afternoon, over 60 miles away. Made 150 miles in the last 24 hours, a big days work for us. Tonight it has been showery and all the wind has died away. So we may not be up to the Island until tomorrow unless we get a breeze soon. The time seems to be very long to me, having nothing to do and I often long to be on deck working about. But as Captain I must not do so.

Monday 3rd.
A dead calm and still not past the Island. Not moved all day; sun very hot.

Thursday Sept. 6th.
We still keep crawling our way South and today we have got in sight of the Canary Islands, Palma and Tenerife. But it has been cloudy over the land and we could not see the peak of Tenerife, which is a great height. Of course we are a very long way off, fully 60 miles. What little breeze we have is dead ahead, so we are going away from the Islands now.

This little apprentice boy of ours is growing smaller; he has not got used to salt meat yet. The other lads are all growing useful.

I think I am growing very lazy; I keep wanting to go round the decks and work a bit. I always stay up till midnight or after and seldom sleep before 2 o'clock, always waking up at daylight for coffee at 5 o'clock. I try to have a sleep between that and 8 o'clock, but seldom do so. But I always do a little sleep in the afternoon between 2 and 4 and I suppose that spoils my night for me.

Sunday 9th.
This is our 4th Sunday at sea and again we have the Brierholme in company. Passed her again yesterday but she still keeps well up to us and a large ship with her.

We have got the NE Trade winds at last and so are going on our way rejoicing, but not very fast yet. We hope they will increase soon and take us well past the Cape Verdes, letting us get across the Equator in something under 40 days.

The Ladas still keeps up her name, as there is no-one passed us yet. A French Barque passed us the other day when it was nearly calm, but when we got a breeze we soon passed her again, leaving her out of sight astern. The Brierholme keeps up best with us of any yet.

Monday 10th September.
A ship called the Hilston, of London, has overtaken us today; is alongside now at 8pm and the Brierholme out of sight behind again. We are just gliding along, very easy at 5 or 6 miles an hour, very fine clear weather and a smooth sea. I took off my shirt to sew on some buttons and when I put it on again, I found that I had put one on the wrong side. Martha has gone and starched my old shirt collars, so I had to take one off yesterday. It was so stiff I could not bend my neck with it on, so I will have to wash it out.

Wednesday 12th.
We have quite a fleet of vessels about us today; three big ships, one with four masts and they have all overtaken us last night. The other ship has gone clean away out of sight ahead and if these others do the same, we must be getting slower surely; or else want more wind. We are painting the ship around white inside now, while the fine weather lasts.

I often turn round when I hear someone speak about the Mate, quite forgetting that I am the Master now. I have read Pearson's Weeklies until I am tired of them; they all seem as if none of you had opened them.

Thursday 13th
I am quite out of countenance with the Ladas today. Two ships have passed us and two Barques are keeping up with us; we have a nice breeze too. One German ship from Cardiff for Port of Santos, 23 days out and we are 26. I can not brag about the Ladas being fast now.

Saturday 15th.
Well we have had two days run, 177 miles each day. Now we are stopped, with a faint breeze from ahead and a dozen ships all round us. All the ships, fast and slow, are here together now. Some going

one way and some another, crossing. We are 4 weeks out today and I shall be glad if we get across the Equator in another 10 days. I have no dog and no Mrs O'Neill to write about and I think my days drag along in weary fashion, I am getting very lazy, but not fat. At any rate, I do not sleep much. I lay tossing about from midnight until 5 o'clock, when the Steward brings me a cup of coffee. Then I lay about until 7 or half-past and get up tired of my sleeping mattress. In fact I generally lay on the sofa after coffee.

Our hens have never layed any eggs yet. They are getting thin, as we have no grub for them and they won't eat rice.

Sunday 16th.
A very hot day, thermometer at 82 degrees, with the awning spread over the Poop. A very faint NE air all day, just moving along a couple of knots and a lot of vessels about. We are all slow alike now. Some of the sailors have been showing their goodness tonight by singing Sankey's hymns. I am hoping to get a freshening of the NE Trades to carry us a bit further on our way, for a day or so at any rate.

Sunday September 23rd.
Another Sunday makes the 6th from Maryport and we are not at the Equator yet, but hope we have got hold of the tail-end of the SE Trades, as it is blowing a nice breeze now.

I have been wondering where you went for your Band of Hope trip, if you have had it yet; I hope it was enjoyable. Uncle John's chickens are getting very thin; they are saucy and won't eat scarce any of the stuff we have to offer them. Rice, barley or peas and tatie peelings. So I have two killed every week and eat them, but our potatoes are getting scarce now, though they have kept well so far. I have a very good Cook and Steward, in fact a good crew through-out and so far we have been very happy and comfortable. But the time seems long to me and I think I will be getting fat soon like Uncle John. I never walk about long enough to make my leg ache now, as it used to last voyage.

I have been looking at every ship to see if it is the Dunboyne, catching up to us, as she might easy do while we had so many calms. She would sail faster than us at any rate. One of our boys has had a very bad toe, but it is improving now. The little boy we have sings like a little girl, all the latest songs of the day.

Sunday 30th.
Well we passed the island of Fernando Noronha, about 10 miles away. It has a very peculiar peak or pyramid and it just looks for all the world like a very large church or cathedral. The peak is exactly like a spire, a very high one, as it is 800 feet high. The old descriptions say it is a very lovely and fruitful island, but used as a convict settlement by the Brazilians.

Well we keep just toiling on our way, with beautiful fine weather all this week. But if the wind does not shift soon by tomorrow, we will have to go back East, as we will be on top of the coast by noon. There is another rock called the Roccas some 70 miles from the other island, with a light house on it, but we are too far off to see it.

The sun has been burning my ears today, as I have not got a hat to keep it off; it was left in the Dunboyne. A big steam boat passed today and I hoisted my numbers; but if he reports us, Uncle Joe would not know the flags and the name is not in the book. We passed one of the Sydney passenger ships close this afternoon, the Macquairie. I knew her before when she was the Melbourne, going to Melbourne. The Mate has just come down to say she (the ship) is coming up all the time, that is getting nearer her proper course. If she only comes up, I shall be very thankful. We covered over 200 miles in distance yesterday, but only 120 of it was the right way; the rest we would rather have done without.

Sunday 7th October.
Well we have got away South a bit now, but were much humbugged the first 3 days of the week beating off the land and it delayed us very much; but the last 3 days we have done good work, making nearly 600 miles. But now the wind has fallen light and we are getting along only slowly; hope it will not fall calm altogether.

We will soon be getting down into cold weather now by next Sunday. Hope it will be a deal cooler, as we will probably be abreast of the River Plate (Rio la Plata). A little Barque is keeping us company today; now the wind is light, anything can keep up with us. The Ladas wants plenty of wind to drive her. I do not think she would sail with the Dunboyne at all.

Our chickens are getting less daily, now only two left and they are also getting very tough. So the Cook has to curry them to make them eatable. Hope we will have better winds to Cape Horn from here than last voyage.

Sunday 14th.

It is a deal cooler today, as we have a strong wind from the South (right ahead) and had a nasty rainy morning of it before it became fine in the forenoon. We are yet a long way from the River Plate and will not make much progress if this wind is going to last. The Ladas has shown her stern to a couple of Barques this afternoon, left them very fast. But as we are not going the right way, it is not much good sailing fast. We killed the last of the hens today; the poor things did not enjoy life on board ship and I am glad we have got the last eaten up.

I have not got quite used to my spring mattress and I hardly will, for when we get rough seas I will have it taken off; for it is bad enough for the ship to roll one about without the mattress doing so too.

Sunday 21st October.

Here we have been stuck with a head wind the last two days, but at last we have got past the mouth of the Plate. I hope the wind will soon change and let us get on South to Cape Horn. We had some strong winds last week and the ship behaves very well. It is getting very cold now with this South wind.

Sunday October 28th.

My Dear Daughter, another Sunday night and we are driving on to get past the Falkland Islands. There has been a strong gale all day and many hail squalls. Now I feel the ship heeling over to another one; but the Ladas is a good ship and can stand some sail on her. As we are only 30 miles or so off the land, the sea is smooth and she is not putting her bows under water as she did this morning. Yesterday we were driving on to pass outside the islands, but the wind shifted this morning, so now we are pass-

61

ing the other side of them.

The weather is getting a bit cold now and I had to set the boys to get their hands and faces washed. Evidently they think that dirt keeps them warm; for blackness they could shame a collier. I do not feel so cold now; my room here is warmer than it was in the old ship and I have not yet lit the cabin fire.

We are 71 days out today and are almost sure to be over the 100 getting to Corral, but we can not help it if the wind keeps dead in our teeth the whole time. I am making my way as fast as I can. Hoping you are all well at home,   Goodnight.

Monday 29th.

A very fine day today and this evening we were very much surprised to fall in with a very large iceberg. Took it for the fog bank for a long time. Had it been dark, I might have got very close to it before seeing it. In fact I was not looking for one so near the land and what the Mate took for land this morning could have been ice too. As the wind changed, I had to turn the ship away from the ice. It was after tacking ship that I found out it was ice; I was merely taking it for a fog bank. So now we are going away South to the land, which is only 60 miles or so off.

Tuesday 30th October.

Well last night we were stopped going one way for ice; and at daylight this morning I was afraid I was going to have to go back from the land, as we were getting close to the small islands, where the tide runs through them and around at about 6 miles an hour. Fortunately the wind freshened and came more favourable, so we got clear of them, but then nearly ran on top of a small low island a few feet above the water. That was just at 8 o'clock; the fair wind only lasted an hour, then shifted right ahead. At 3 o'clock this afternoon we had to turn around away from some more islands. Now we can go West for 200 miles or so. We are making some zig-zags in our courses. Now the wind is partly favourable; if it lasts till noon tomorrow, by then we may have a change.

Wednesday 31st.

Beautiful and calm all forenoon. A large seal is playing round the ship, popping up like a jack-in-the-box and snorting as much as to say 'Here I am'. Then it would tumble over on its side and go down like a shot; we could see it in the clear water many fathoms down. At 8 pm now we have a fine breeze, going 10 knots an hour, making for some Straits I am going to pass through, if the wind holds good as it is.

Thursday 8 pm.

Well we came down to the Straits in great style last night, getting inside by 9 this morning. Just in the middle of them, our breeze dropped and came out right ahead for us but very faint. So I just thought the tide would take us out again. After about an hour, the wind came fair for us again and we have managed to crawl through slowly until we are about 12 miles outside now and I hope we will keep our breeze and it will increase.

November 2nd 1894.

Well we had a little fair wind all night and ought to have been at Cape Horn nearly by noon, but were nearly 20 miles off by our time. We saw it at 1 o'clock and are nearly abreast of it now. The wind is ahead and it is a dirty rainy night, so we have been snugging down a bit. I do not expect it will be very bad, but there is a very big sea against us all nigh. Today she is taking some twists, enough to throw me away from my desk. Still, we have warm weather; have not had the cabin fire lit yet.

Saturday 3rd.

The ship has been putting some fantastic twists out of herself today and last night, but as she was doing some good at last, I let her have all sail; she never put any water on deck at all. It has got quite fine again now and we are making tracks back North again. Still a good amount of sea up. Just 77 days from home today and we can easily get out by 90, if we get a small show at all.

Tuesday 6th November.

After much unsettled weather, at last it has wound up with a burst from the SW this forenoon. So tonight the ship is doing some of her worst tricks, tossing things about lively. A boy and a man are laid up with getting knocked down by the ship tumbling and seas coming over. Still, she is going along wonderfully well, considering the wind and sea there is. I hope we will soon run into warmer weather, going straight North.

Sunday November 11th.
I am in hopes of being able to send you this letter this week, as we are only 420 miles off Valdivia now. Unfortunately at present the wind is very much ahead and we are going away from our Port; I do not care to go any nearer the shore than we are.

We are getting up into a little warmer weather now, but have had nothing but hard blows this last week. Moderate for a few hours, then increasing again to a half gale. But on the whole we have had a very favourable passage round the Horn, no very bad weather at all, but always making progress more or less daily. So I have every hope of making a decent passage.

I suppose it will be beginning to get frosty a bit now at home. Does Aunt H. like her spot at Wigton; I wonder if she stops on there. It makes me sick to think of the stopping on spell we are likely to have at Corral here; fully three months. I expect we will have time to get answers to our letters here.

At any rate, it is coming on to blow here and drizzly rain also. So goodnight.

Monday.
It has been blowing hard all day and raining also. Now at dark the wind has dropped to a light breeze, but the rain is falling faster than ever. I am disappointed that the wind has not come fair for us before now We only made about 45 miles this last 24 hours and it is rather annoying to me to be stopped here at the end of my passage. I hope you are progressing well with your music and that you like it.

Wednesday night.
Well we have a nice fair wind at present, which I hoped would have put us into Corral tomorrow. But it is falling light now, so I have no hopes of getting there before Friday at soonest. I was very much annoyed at noon today, when I found the ship had been set back

about 30 miles the 24 hours before. I thought we would have done a fair days work; I hope we will not be served the same this 24 hours, for we have had a fine breeze all day.

Our little apprentice got his arm hurt and laid up, so I let him have two days rest. Then I fetched him on deck and I think he forgot which arm it was, as I saw him using both freely enough. I think he is getting smaller, but the other boys are all getting bigger.

The Mate assures me that this morning at about 7 o'clock he, as well as the rest of his watch, saw a greenness in the water ahead of the ship which proved to be an immense snake. The ship passed it, not her own length off and it appeared to be as long as from the Miz Mast to the Forward House, as thick as the spar on deck; that is 60 feet long and 6 feet thick around. I tell him he should write an account of it to Pearson's Weekly and call it 'The Sea Serpent Again'. He says all the birds were seated on the water and looking at it in a very puzzled way, as it left a greenness in the water behind it. I am quite sorry he did not call me to see it, but the ship was going 9 knots at the time and he was right forward when he saw it; before he could get aft, it was past.

We have made just half the distance to our Port; still 100 miles off and now calm.

Saturday 17th November

Got anchored here all right before noon, just making an even 13 weeks of it. I tried to come in last night and got in the Bay a bit, but the wind came round against me, so I went out again and stopped out all night. This is a very quiet snug little place, very little of a town, only a few wood shanties built up. A wood church, but no priest; no Protestant church at all. We have to go and look for anyone here, no-one seems to come off to the ship at all. I just had to go after the butcher for fresh meat. I could not send a telegram home from here, because they do not know what to charge and would have to send off to Valdivia to know, making an additional expense.

There are more ships here than I expected to see, but only coasters loading wood for Valparaiso. It is all hills and woods around here. The houses are all hid from each other by trees and scrub. No letters down to Corral for the ship; may be some in Valdivia.

Barque Ladas, Corral.   December 9th, 1894.

My Dear Daughter,
We have now been here over three weeks and are not yet one third discharged. It is quite evident we will be here fully six weeks or two months more. But as we are not yet fixed to go anywhere alse, it does not matter much. By the time we are ready, we may get wheat at Taleahuano and I hope we do. I went up to Valdivia the other evening and stopped until the following evening. The streets are just terrible where the carts go along. In the wet weather, they get up to the axles in mud. But just now they are dry and hard, as it has been fine for a week or more. Still, the town is situated in a very pretty place. The river is a good width across and it ought really to be a rising place. There are a good many breweries and distilleries along the river side. A large flour mill and distillery was burnt to the ground the other night. I saw the glare of it down here in Corral, as I was walking the deck at 10 o'clock at night.

Everybody drinks beer here, any amount of it and I find it difficult to make the people understand what a teetotaller is. The idea of anyone being foolish enough to not drink unlimited beer when he has the chance to do so seems to astonish them immensely. The people are mostly Germans and of German descent and there are not any English schools here; only German and native ones and the people have to learn German as well as the Spanish that the Natives talk.

During 10 months of the year here, they have a terrible amount of rain around this South of Chile. It is only the next two months they can depend on any fine weather. For the first fortnight we were here, it rained more or less every day; but last week was fine and the potatoes are now growing fast a few are in the market; I got some new ones in Valdivia. The beef is cheap here; they sell it about 2d. a pound.

It is a very quiet little place Corral, but very pretty; hills all around, covered with all kinds of bushes, but no large trees. It is quite impossible to walk through the scrub, it is so thick. Even the inside of caves and precipices are covered with ferns and briers, hanging down from the sides and roof.

Another English vessel has arrived today from London, 90 days and a Maryport man is Captain of her, Captain Briscoe. He sailed many years for Ritsons. I remember him when we were lads serving our time, but he said he could not remember me. The only amusement we get here is to go ashore of an afternoon and talk with a German woman who keeps the Hotel and has just got her niece out from Hamburg. They talk English very funny, but want to learn it better. The mistress is a widow and is going to marry the Captain of a steamboat, a second cousin of hers very soon.

Barque Ladas, Corral.　　　　*Sunday Night, December 23rd.*

My Dear Daughter,
I am not near enough to you to send you a Christmas greeting, but you will know that I wish you every joy all the same. Well I received your letters at last, after beginning to think you had forgotten me altogether at Crosby and I would have to cultivate some fresh friends here. So they have made a pupil teacher of you at the school. I suppose while doing so you are not neglecting your own schooling. I am not surprised the master should want to know if you could not get a pair of slippers to wear in school, as you would make a clattering noise walking about in clogs.

Everybody about here are decorating up for Christmas and any amount of bushes are being sent to Valdivia from here. Today things have been looking lively on the little wharf here. Two steamboats called in, so all the small boats were down from Valdivia with passengers. I got all the carpets put down in the cabins for Christmas and all the glasses and decanters round the cabin. I told the Steward today that the decanter looked very queer standing empty and he had better put some weak tea in it to make it look like wine and he has actually done so. So I can invite people to have a glass of wine and they will be surprised to find that it is tea; very weak at that. It will take us another three weeks to get all our cargo out of the ship and another week to get ballast in.

Christmas Eve.
I have been on shore to see the 'fine' tree they have up at the hotel, hung with all sorts of fancy gilt things and lots of little candles they

were going to light at dark. But I would not stop to see the effect,
, as it was 8 o'clock and I get the boat hoisted up at that time. Our
boys were getting some bushes to put up at the mast head in the
morning.

Christmas Day
And many happy returns of the day to you my dear daughter. I
hope you are enjoying a fine time of it at Crosby. Well the boys got
the ship decorated with a bush or two, just to give a festive appearance to the Ladas. We are the only one that has done so. I gave some
of my men leave on shore this afternoon and two of them have
failed to come off. Got drunk and gone to sleep somewhere no
doubt.

December 26th.
Four of the sailors drunk yet. One came out on deck and jumped
right over the side, swam to the nearest ship and stopped there a
couple of hours. Then he jumped overboard from there and swam
back again. I went up to Valdivia in the evening, but every place
was shut up. Everybody was keeping Christmas up.

Well we are getting on with our cargo slowly but surely, but there
is now need to hurry, as we will likely have a week or two's idleness
before we get fixed to load anywhere. I hope we will go no further
than Talcahuano, just 200 miles or so from here and load wheat
there. But before you get this at Crosby, you will know from Mr
Ritson what we are doing. At present, everything is very dull out
here and freights are getting lower every day.

Sunday Evening.
I have just been on board the Barque 'Ivanhoe' to service this
evening. Captain Briscoe has some mission books and holds a
service on Sundays. So I took the boys across and joined in with
them this evening. His sailors would not come to service, because
he did not let them go ashore today and get drunk as mine did on
Christmas Day.

The time seems very long lying here and what cargo we get out
seems so little. This week we lost Christmas Day and the day after
and next week we will probably lose two days also. The only

consolation is that, if all the cargo was out, we would not know then what next to do or where to go. But we could at least get the ship painted round outside.

The new potatoes are now getting well in, but are very dear for this country, about 15 pence a stone. The old ones are very bad and dear also; really not much cheaper than the new ones when all the bad ones are picked out. The seemingly good ones are also bad inside, so that our potato bill will amount to a respectable sum before we leave here.

The bathing season will soon commence here. They come down from Valdivia for a salt water dip. I saw a few were having one today and, as there are no such things as bathing boxes, they had to utilise a large sheet to undress and dress under in full view of all the ships in the Port. But I notice that some enterprising individual was busy building a rude hut on the sand for a dressing room and will probably make a good thing of it charging a few cents for the use of it.

A speculative youngster the other day came to us with a few roses and was given a ten cent piece (a penny). Since then we are invariably offered flowers by all the youngsters in the place, as we are getting well known about here now. I think that the oldest inhabitant in Corral has never seen so many ships in the place at once; there are actually seven sailing ships here, so business must be booming.

For the present I must conclude, as it is now bed time and the mail goes tomorrow. So with best love to you, I remain Your Loving Father,   *T. Messenger.*

Kind regards to Aunt H. and Grandfather and Mother, also to Mr and Mrs Richardson and their girls. Here, I can't find anyone kind enough to play and sing for me.

Barque Ladas, Corral.   *January 20th 95.*

My Dear Daughter,
You will likely know that we have been ordered to go to Newcastle, New South Wales. I am trying to get away from here as quick as I can, but will not be able to do so for at least 8 or 9 days; probably

more, as there is some delay in bringing ballast along.

As soon as you receive this, you can write to Newcastle and I will get the letters there. I fully expect to be about 70 or 80 days going there. If you look at the map in school, you will see it is a long way back round Cape Horn and round the Cape of Good Hope and thence around Tasmania. A long dreary passage; I would much rather have loaded here at Talcahuano, or any other Port on the coast here.

We will likely have to come back to the West Coast here with coals, or else to San Francisco, so we will make a long voyage of it anyways. I still have 120 rails in the ship, but may get rid of them tomorrow. A large steamer from Maryport is discharging rails here also, but as he has plenty of steam and large hatches, he will soon get away; probably before I do so yet.

We can get a decent potato now; the new ones are fully in the market. The only other English ship that was here, the Ivanhoe (Capt. Briscoe of Maryport) left last Thursday, so I have lost my company and I miss him some. The Captain of the steamer I don't often see.

Today is like the return of Winter here again, although it has stopped raining now and the sun is out. You must give my kind love to all friends; and with love to yourself, hoping you are quite well, I remain you Father,   *T. Messenger.*

Barque Ladas, Corral.   *January 95.*

My Dear Daughter,
As I will soon be leaving for Newcastle now, I must first send you this one more letter before I go. I could have been away today but I was stopped, waiting further orders. Some people here said they had received a cablegram from my owners, to tell me to stop in Corral. So after getting all ready for sea, I sent a telegram home yesterday morning and got the answer back this afternoon to go to Newcastle same as before. So perhaps the people in Valparaiso had misunderstood the telegram. I am sorry if it is so, as I might have been away to sea today, but it is too late to do anything now.

Sunday 3rd.

We are getting the weather very hot in the daytime here now, but the nights so far have kept cool and pleasant. The people have all come down to Corral to bathe and every house is occupied. I was going to say from top to bottom, but they are nearly all single story places; I should say from end to end. At present in one part of the Bay, they are nearly driven out of their homes by the stench from vast numbers of cuttle fish thrown up on the beach a day or two ago, which the people are too lazy to bury. They say that last year they were piled up 3 feet deep on the beach and the people were compelled to carry them to sea and throw them overboard. The folks had to leave their houses.

We had some young Englishmen here the other day from Valparaiso. They were school teachers and during the holiday they came South for a trip and were at the hotel here for a few days. They seemed to thoroughly enjoy themselves around Corral, as there is plenty of places of interest around here in the old Forts. There is no less than seven of them at various points around the Bay and the old guns and shot are still lying around.

I hope your Grandfather and Grandmother are enjoying good health, as it will be cold weather with you now and I hope you are also all right. I am pleased to say that I have kept quite well all the time here, but will be glad to get away to a fresh place; we have been here too long.

Everybody admires the Ladas very much here, but they are not as forward as they are in Australia in coming aboard. They might be if we were alongside a wharf.

I am wondering if you are tired of teaching yet, or if Mr. Marsh is not yet tired of you; probably the children are.

With kind love to you and don't forget or lose the address. I remain your Father,   *T. Messenger.*

(Write to; Barque Ladas, R.B.Wallace, Newcastle, N.S.W. Australia).

71

CORRAL TO NEWCASTLE N.S.W., AUSTRALIA

Barque Ladas, Lat.43 S, Long.86 W.   *1895.*

My Dear Daughter,
We are now over 8 days from Corral and although we have gone
over a good amount of distance, it has unfortunately not been in a
direct line. Yesterday at noon I was just back abreast of the place we
started from; only 500 miles off. We have the choice of two routes
for Newcastle; to go round across the Pacific ocean in fine weather,
or down round Cape Horn in stormy weather. So when we left Port,
we got a fine strong South wind and I thought to go North (Pacific
route). for 3 days we had a fine run out of the land. Then after a short
calm a fine NW wind sprung up and I said here's a splendid chance
to go South and away we went spanking for 12 hours. Then a good
hard squall or two and the wind shifted to the South again. I was
very much annoyed and hardly knew what to do, but thought I
would compromise the matter and go out West, so I did. Only the
very big sea sent me North also. Then I had another days calm
nearly and the wind backed into the North again, so I set off before
it again for Cape Horn. As I have had a couple of days run South,
I think I shall not try the North route again. But I was very much
exasperated at the fickle wind, heading me which ever way I went.
Now the wind has gone into the SW again, but I shall go on South
now and take my chance of a passage this way. I have not really lost
much time yet; getting so far out West has made this a fair wind for
me so far.

Sunday Night.
This is the second one from Corral and it has been a fine day but too
calm, as we could not get along any until this evening. A fine breeze
has sprung up and we are now travelling on down South for Cape
Horn. We have been getting on fairly well. The weather was a little

unsettled last night, but not bad; it ended up being too fine and taking all the wind away. We have not made the weather much colder yet, though we are getting well South; but we will find it so when we near the Cape, which I hope to do in 4 days more. Now I am only about 200 miles off the Cape and have a fine pleasant breeze and no cold weather yet.

After all my bother at the beginning of the passage, I have made a fair run to the Cape after all and now I hope to keep it up for a matter of six weeks. A long time and a long dreary run before us, but it is a fine time of the year for it. Last night the ship did tumble about in a very uneasy manner. I had to get up and put more clothes on the bed, as I felt cold around my shoulders; old age again.

22nd February.
Passed the Cape this morning. This afternoon signalled the Inversnaid of Aberdeen, 1312 tons, from Melbourne to London 34 days out. The Captain asked if the ship was new and when he got the name, he hoisted up signal letters to say 'horse'. For a little time I could not make out what he meant, but it dawned upon me at last; the Derby winner, Ladas.

Well we have left him a long way behind us now and he will think the ship is as good as the horse also.

23rd Feb.
I just got nicely to sleep at 1 o'clock this morning, when the water came through the deck and dropped onto my face. It woke me up soon and I had to clear out on to the sofa. Calm fine weather all day today.
Sunday 24th.
Have had a very fine day until this evening at 6 o'clock, when it became stormy and we have now a fesh gale and plenty of rain driving us on our way East. My greatest anxiety now is about ice. I don't want to get too friendly with the icebergs down South here. So I have to go carefully at night-time and keep a good look out. (Gale died away to a light breeze before morning).

Thursday 26th.
Have had a nice run for two days and promising well for a third one so far. So we are steadily making the distance shorter and have

73

escaped the ice so far. The ship did roll and tumble about this afternoon. I could not lie on the sofa; she rolled me off. I have quite a job to keep warm in bed and we have not any cold weather yet and should not have for at least another month. Then we should be well through with our journey; I wish it was over and I am thankful we have been favoured with fine weather so far.

February 27th, 10pm.
Are doing some good work now, a splendid fresh fair wind and clear sky. Going between 11 and 12 knots, sea very smooth. Passed South georgia 60 miles off today.

28th Feb.
Breeze gave out before noon today, so did not get a big run, only 220 miles. Two very large whales about this forenoon, one close to the ship showed a back as broad as the ship and a tail about 20 feet across I should say. As it threw it out of the water it looked a terrible size and I thought I wouldn't have liked to be in a boat near it and had a smack from it. It would have been decidedly unpleasant.

Friday March 1st.
All last night I was quite disgusted that we were having such a light breeze, little thinking that it was for our good that it was so. Had it been strong we might easily, or almost surely, have been against the ice. At 8 o'clock this morning discovered a field of ice on the lee beam and, as we sailed on, I found it was right round ahead and we could not get past it the way we were going. So at 10 o'clock I put the ship about and came back again to pass round the other end of it and kept sailing on round it, from one bay to another as it proved. For at 7 o'clock we found the ice showing up all around up ahead again and I had to put about again, as it was getting dark and I dare not risk sailing on in the dark. So now I am just dodging along waiting for daylight, when I hope to be able to get away clear of it. A mercy it keeps fine weather.

Saturday 2nd.
Another very fine day and have got a breeze from the opposite

direction, that is North. Have been travelling along in good style all afternoon; only saw one piece of ice at noon today. I supposed it was the very same piece we were close to last night when I put about. The wind is increasing all the time and we are going fast, so I am very anxious about getting near any more ice. I am keeping everybody on the watch for it and longing for morning to come.

Tuesday 5th March.
For two days now we have been sailing through icebergs; very fine weather though. Yesterday there were half a dozen bergs around us. We got clear of them before night and thought we would see no more. But at daylight this morning they were more numerous than ever and this evening we got amongst quite a school of them and had to be careful steering amongst them, for a lot of pieces were just level with the water. We seem to have got clear of them by dark, or got into an open space. At any rate I am sailing on carefully, hoping to meet none tonight. It has come on a bit rainy and dirty and the wind same as we had it Sunday, for it rained all that day. I am sorry we are not making very rapid progress along here, though we have fine weather.

Wednesday 6th.
The wind came fair for us after midnight and I had to let her run and risk the ice. I am glad to say we saw none until daylight, when the wind freshened to a strong gale; we have been tearing along 13 knots all day, passing a good few icebergs. I shall be glad when we get clear of them. Tonight it is fine and clear and the moon shining brightly; had not seen it before, though it is now ten days old.

I could not sleep any last night, for a knock in the dark at one of these icebergs would send us to the bottom like a stone. We are still travelling along at 10-12 knots and passing occasional pieces of ice; none of it very big though. Made a good run this day after all, 210 miles.

Friday 8th.
A beautiful day and the ocean this afternoon was dotted with icebergs glistening in th sunshine. Pieces away on the horizon we

could just see like a point of light and the shapes many of them had taken were many and fantastic. One piece like a perfect square block; another like Dutch barn covered with snow, appearing full up with hay. The lower ice having a darker appearance, as if the top or eaves overlapped it. But the most common shape seems to be a church with more or less of a spire on them. They look very grand and imposing on a calm and sunshiny day, as today had been. But with a cloudy dark night and the ship travelling 10 knots, they are most welcome a long way off. They are as plentiful as ever around us and I hope we get no thick bad weather until we are well clear of them.

Saturday Night.
A wild stormy rainy night and the wind fair dead ahead at East since last evening. One consolation, we have seen no ice since noon today and I hope we will see no more. The head wind has done so much for us, it has driven us out from the ice. But now we are tired of it and want a fair wind. Possibly we may get it before morning. The ship is kicking about too much to write easy, so will give it up, with my love to you at home.

Sunday Night.
And just the opposite to last night. Now we have a faint wind right behind us and foggy all day, although it has cleared a bit now. The gale dropped after daylight and the wind shifted fair. So we have made a little progress all day, though very slowly. So I am really getting disgusted with it; 3 days and done almost nothing.

Tuesday March 12th.
Latitude 47 10S, Long 11 10. Nice breeze and very fine weather, going along easily on our way. The fog had partly cleared away and we do not see any ice about, so we hope we have got clear of it at last. The Steward complained today that the boys had taken some of his suet and had been cooking it on their stoves. Making dumplings no doubt. I told him he should not hang it up in their way, as mischievous boys can not keep their fingers off things. But I took their stove away from them so, if they steal any more, they will have to eat it raw.

I have been quite disgusted today to find my nose breaking out again. The cold amongst the ice was too much for it likely, so we just got away from it in time, or it might have been a deal worse.

I was just reading the story of Perry Cass in the West Cumberland Times Christmas number. I remember your mother was a little frightened of him when he was coming round Crosby with his rag bag and was doubtful whether he might not have had a hand in stealing your Uncle John's clothes from the wash-house there.

Only 6000 more miles to Newcastle; what a long way.

Wednesday 13th.

I was just about to go to bed at 4 o'clock last night after writing up this log to you and congratulating myself with a nice breeze, a fine moonlight night and no ice about (I thought), when the Mate came down and said he could see a number of icebergs about. So I rushed up on deck and sure enough here we were sailing right up amidst them. As I was afraid of going through them in the dark, I decided to go back the way I came in, as the wind allowed me to do so. I got out into the open sea again and at daylight ran through the openings between the bergs. A lot of very big ones and very high they were too. As soon as we got clear of them, the wind fell away to a calm; now it has come on a dense fog again. Had it been a foggy night last night, we would surely have gone against one of those big bergs. One of them today, about 300 ft high, seemed composed of square blocks built up pyramid fashion, as those glass ornaments are. The top piece seemed as if a breeze would blow it over. What a mercy we are having such fine weather amongst all this ice, though I am grumbling at getting along so slowly. Again at midnight we passed a lot of big bergs.

Friday 15th March.

Well we do not seem to be able to find any good winds to help us on our way now. We did get 190 miles from noon yesterday to noon today, but we had a miserable time of it driving through rain and fog, never knowing if we might be alongside an iceberg any minute. I was glad when it cleared up and we could see a bit. Only saw two bergs today, so they are a bit more scarce now. One today we were going straight for and, if it had been a foggy night, could easy have struck it. Tonight it has settled down thick fog again, but as we have no wind it does not matter much.

Sunday 17th.
Same foggy weather all the time and more or less ice. From 10 o'clock last night to three this afternoon, saw no ice and I thought we might be getting out of it. But no, all at once we saw seven icebergs and, by appearances, likely more about the way the barometer is rising. I am getting quite an expert amongst icebergs. By watching the glass I can almost tell when we are nearing any great lot of ice.

Yesterday we managed a nice little run of 180 miles, but now it is calm nearly, so we can not hurt the ice much if we do hit it. The Cook complains someone has stolen his clothes and tobacco, so I gave him leave to search the boys place. He say he found nothing but rags in their chests.

I suppose you will be at church or chapel now at Crosby and wondering where your father is. I am sorry to say I am getting on very badly on my way to Newcastle. I came around this way to get good winds and instead we are having gentle breezes and a sea like oil all the way, ever since crossing into East longitude at the Meridian of Greenwich. That is where a line drawn from the North Pole to the South pole passes through Greenwich.

It is very dark and foggy and if we were moving much through the water, I would be very anxious knowing ice to be about.

20th March.
On the Monday morning at daylight after the fog cleared and we got a breeze, we found ourselves right in the thick of a vast number of icebergs. Fortunately the wind got fresher and the sky cleared, so we could pick our way through them. But for 4 hours, they were just thick enough for anything. Ever since we have been going along in good style, passing through lots of it, until today when it seems to be a little clearer. It is also a deal warmer. We have to keep a very sharp lookout at night to clear the ice. It is never very clear; we can not see it far off and, going 11-12 knots at times, I have been very anxious these two nights. We have had a few narrow escapes of it. Tonight there is less about. Still I know it is about and conse-

quently as anxious as ever, the breeze being half a gale at times.

Sunday March 24th.
We have been making some good days work this last week, having gone over 1500 miles since last Sunday. This has altered our time considerably; we are now over 4 hours ahead of you at home. So you will be preparing for church or chapel now; we are nearly 10 o'clock.

I am glad to say we are clear of ice for a few days now and hope we meet no more of it. Our days now are getting shorter very fast and the moon is done, but we have been clear of fog also since we cleared the ice. So I have not been so anxious these last few nights, though we are going sometimes over 11 knots. I must not reckon my chickens before they are hatched, but I would like to be in Newcastle by this day three weeks. Now we have got into a fine run of winds, I hope we may carry them along with us.

Monday 25th.
Our breeze has been very light all day, but has shifted round NW and is freshening up, so we may do a good days run again. Got 230 miles last 24 hours up until noon today and hope to get over 200 miles again tomorrow. I think all hands were trying to catch birds this afternoon. There were so many about, from stormy petrels to large albatrosses and some splendid molly hawks. No one got any, though they dropped on the water alongside.

Wednesday 27th March.
Have had another two days good run of 230 miles each, but this next one is going to be short by the shape of the wind so far. We do not fall in with any more ice and I hope we will not, as we have made a fine run since we got clear of it.

Wednesday April 3rd.
Quite a full week since I have written anything to my little girl at home. In fact the ship has been going so fast and rolling so much that once or twice I got prepared to write but could not hold on, so put it off to a more suitable time. But as she still keeps going and rolling away cheerily, I have at last set to, to do or die. In other

words write something or get rolled out of my chair in trying.

Well this week we have run the distances of 200, 186, 204, 264, 274, 210 and 280, the best days run this last 24 hours she has ever run yet. Only that the wind fell light at daylight, we would have got a good 300 miles out of the Ladas. We passed the end of Australia yesterday at noon and are well on the way across the Great Australian Bight. Another three days run like the last would put us right across, then we have another 500 miles to go to Newcastle, making 1500 miles to go yet. We are now 55 days out; if I get in before the 65 days, I will think I have done well.

We have seen no more ice, but the Southern Lights for the last three nights have been very bright; almost like the illumination from a large electric light. I am often startled when I hear a noise or shout on deck, thinking the lookout is reporting ice and in my dreams I am constantly sailing through it. However we are now safe from that peril, for this passage at any rate.

Sunday 7th April.
Now we have a dead head wind; only it will take us along past Tasmania, or Van Dieman's Land as it used to be called when I went to school. We are not 200 miles off it now, with a strong breeze and the weather quite warm and mild these last few days. If I reach past Tasmania tomorrow, that will make 60 days passage for us there, which after all is very good and I hope she will not spoil it by taking a week from there to Newcastle. I meant to have gone through Bass's Straits between Tasmania and Australia, as it would cut off a bit of distance, but I am not likely to get that way now as it is no nearer from where we are at present. I shall be glad to get the ship into Newcastle, as I am tired of this passage though, barring the ice, it has been a fine weather passage all the way.

Tuesday 9th.
Sighted the Tasmanian land at 4 o'clock this afternoon and find we are just correct with our position. Today the Ladas had been doing a fantastic fling with herself. She jumps on top of a sea and being so light she comes down flop on top of it, sending the water flying on both sides. As the wind shifted with a hard squall and thunder and lightning this morning, we are heading the old sea, caused by the

head wind we had the last two days. Thus getting the chance to do some good and put her to it. In the squalls she is just lively; makes people get hold with one hand before loosening the other. I slide across my room like on a skating rink. Sometimes, like the present time, it gets fine and moderate and she goes easy. We are just 600 miles from Newcastle now and may get in before Sunday, if are lucky.

Thursday Night April 11th.
We are running along on our way rejoicing to the tune of 11 knots an hour and have been keeping it up pretty well since noon today. This is to make up for it being nearly calm all last night and with this breeze we could be off Newcastle by midnight tomorrow. At any rate, we hope to get in by early on Saturday and have a quiet Sunday reading all our letters from home. Last time I was here, I was longing for letters from your Mother and we arrived on a Sunday morning before breakfast. I had been up all night, so went straight to bed soon as ever we were fast. But the agent brought off the letters, so of course I could not sleep then, but had to read mine; they were the very nicest letters your dear Mother had ever written me. I suppose because she said how she had missed me and how you constantly talked of your Dada. I wonder if she knows how I am thinking and writing about her tonight. May God protect you and bring you up as good and faithful a woman as she was.

My next few lines I hope will be to tell you we are safe in Port.

Sunday Night 10 o'clock.
Well I am disappointed at not getting in by today, but we got off Newcastle all right at daylight yesterday (Saturday) morning and they had the flags up to say that the bar was dangerous to cross. The lifeboat came out to us and said I had better get away to sea again. So I got and the result is I am now 40 miles North of the place and can't get back to it. after beating about all day today and only got a trifle of 10 miles farther away, it seems I am not likely to do any better tomorrow. But I feel comforted that I got reported yesterday and also that I have two vessels more in company in misfortune. You will probably know that I am here by this time, but you won't know that I hear it raining like mischief on deck now.

81

Here is Tuesday night and we are just about as near Newcastle as ever we were on Sunday. We have just been going off and coming back to the same spot. Every time we gain a little, we lose it the next. Now it is a calm and we are 40 miles off still. So when we will get in I do not know. Only one vessel in sight today; been with us since Saturday and keeping about the same distance to windward. The other ones are evidently doing much worse than us, as they have gone clear out of sight.

It is time we were in Port, as all our potatoes are finished and done. I thought if I could only get up to this Point Stephens, 24 miles from Newcastle, the tug boat would come off after us. Yesterday and today I was close to it, but no boat appeared. A fair wind now and we will be there tomorrow.

Saturday 20th April 1895.
Well we managed to get in on Wednesday. The tug boats found us at last and I had two of them offering to tow me in to Port. The one I chose took 5 hours to tow me into the harbour. I got all your home letters all right and I see you have been earning no end of money and been to Maryport to spend it. You omit to mention where your Aunt Hannah is now, if still at Wigton or not. We are going to be here a month at least, so the Colliery people tell me. The mine we get our coal from is only a small one and does not load ships very fast. They have two very large ships to load before us, which would not have been the case had we got right in. I am sorry for it, for in another month it will be fairly Winter. I see you are having some changes about the Moor since I left home.

Kind regards to your Grandfather and Mother and Aunt H. and love to yourself, from your father,   *T. Messenger*

Barque Ladas, Newcastle, N.S.W.   *May 5th 1895.*

My Dear Daughter,
We are now here over a fortnight and have to wait another fortnight yet before we will be loaded. I think Mr Ritson will be fancying we are going to be kept here for good. But every ship is alike, big and small, all kept over a month. I was over on the Blue Mountains at

Katoomba last week and saw all my friends there and they were pleased to see me. We had a very nice time of it visiting all the pretty sights, then spending the evenings with singing and games. We had a good company of nice young people stopping there. Mrs Knight's two sons had been away for 4 days in the bush looking for a missing man, but only found his pipe and socks. He had been down the gully fishing; when they get down, there are few places where they can get up again and have to tramp for miles by the brook side. I am sorry now that I did not stay longer at Katoomba. Then I could have gone and seen some wonderful caves there about 30 miles away in the bush. They are one of the wonders of the world; the Jenolan Caves of New South Wales. The mountains are called Blue because of a blue mist which hangs in the valleys.

I may perhaps take another run to Sydney this next week for a few days, if I can find time and money to do so. Today (Sunday) is a very quiet day here. Stopping on board, the harbour seems so quiet, nothing stirring in it. I must go on shore for a walk or to church this evening.

Trusting your Grandfather and Mother are both well, with kind love to yourself, I remain your loving Father,

T. Messenger

(You must write to Barque Ladas, San Diego, Southern California, U.S.A. in 8 weeks time from now)

Barque Ladas, Newcastle, N.S.W.

My Dear Daughter,

I am just on the eve starting another passage that will take me betwen 60 and 70 days, if not more. I am not likely to be at home yet for another 10 months or more and you will have had another Winter over by that time. It will be Summer up on the Coast when we are there and it is nice at Vancouver in the Summer time. But I may not get there in time and that will be a pity if I can not get a cargo there.

I tumbled down the ladder of the Poop at 12 0'clock last night and it has shaken me up considerably. My ribs have been a little sore all day. I was running about this afternoon, trying to get the ship away to sea, but could not do so. We loaded so quick, only 2 days, that the people could not get their stuff on board in time and their papers in the office. But I will be off at noon tomorrow I dare say. It is as well I did not get away today, as it is a calm and raining heavy.

I hope you are all well about Crosby and Birkby Moor, also at Moor Park and that your parrot is all right. I do not think I could get a good one here if I had any money left to buy one. There seem to be lots of canaries about and they want a good price for them. A pound for bird and cage, so I will not get one for fear it should not sing.

I have not much more to say that will interest you, only a nice trick a cheating shoemaker did today with my crew. You must know that two of them were nearly fighting for the job of patching up all the shoes of the crew. I told them the sailors could employ whom they liked. They chose one and got their repairs done and ordered new shoes and boots and actually signed the bills. Or rather they signed a blank bill and the honest shoemaker filled it up after. So I had bills amounting to £20 and more all ready signed and sent in to the office. If I had got away I would surely have paid them, but not a pair of boots had been sent on board and he had put it on heavy for the repairs also. So you see what cheats there are about.

With kind love to you and many kisses, I am your father,

T. Messenger.

NEW SOUTH WALES TO SAN DIEGO
MAY - AUGUST 1895

Ladas, at sea, South Pacific Ocean.   *May 26th, 1895.*

My Dear Daughter,
This is my second Sunday at sea since leaving Newcastle and I am sorry we are only getting along indifferently well. For the last 24 hours, the wind has been dead against us from the NE, but we have had most lovely weather since we left. I thought we were going to get into the SE Trade winds quite easy and get across the Equator in no time, but this has fooled us. However I trust it will not last long in this direction.

Mrs Knight sent me a telegram from Sydney to say she had got home safe and wished me God speed on my voyage. They were disgusted with the coal dust about Newcastle and the ship was in a mess. They had to walk over heaps of coal to get to the cabin, but were pleased to see the ship. Mrs K. brought me two emu eggs; the emu is a large bird like the ostrich and nearest in size to it. So the eggs are as large as goose eggs. Of course the eggs are empty and an Emu is carved on the shells.

10 o'clock has just rung and as your time is 12 hours less than us, you will be at Sunday school most likely. I am on the opposite side of the globe to you and must wish you Goodnight and God be with us till we meet again.

Tuesday 28th May.
We have crossed into West longitude today and so we will have another Tuesday tomorrow. Then we will be twelve hours behind you at home, instead of being 12 hours ahead. So we have a day more in the year than you do, or if we did not alter our day when we got to England, we would find ourselves a day ahead of you.

The sea has been making me sea sick today, the way she has been jumping into the sea. It has been a rainy, squally, disagreeable day. We have been passing through the Kermadec Islands and must have been near a rock tonight, as it lay in our track, but we have not seen it. In fact it has been so misty we could not see any distance.

The wind has been dead against me for the last three days and sent me back again, making a zig zag of our course on the chart. But it can't be helped; I get on the quickest I can. Just at midnight the wind shifted and is now right behind us and is now only light, not strong enough.

Tuesday again
Had a Barque in company today, the first we have seen since we left Newcastle, but he crossed away SEward and is going for Cape Horn very likely.
Wednesday Night.
A strong breeze and the ship is going very fast. If Mr Ritson was here, he would see how we can carry sail in the Ladas. Everything at the utmost stretch and we are scudding away North at 11 knots an hour.   *T.M.*

June 2nd 1895.
This is our 3rd Sunday out and we have not got on very fast so far. But if we keep up the same average right through to San Diego, we would make a very good passage. At present we are looking for the Trade winds and can't find them. A light breeze from the opposite direction instead and very fine lovely weather, so must be thankful for small mercies. It will now be 7 o'clock Monday morning with you and you will soon be getting up to go school. It is 10 o'clock Sunday night with us, your time being just 11 hours ahead of mine here.

We are now in very warm weather, no covering required at nights now; could be like a South Sea Islander and do without clothes altogether. I suppose you will have got my first letters from Newcastle now and I hope you are able to read them. I wonder if you can follow my route on the map now from Newcastle, across the North end of New Zealand; then up between the Friendly or Tonga Islands and Tahiti, or Otahuiti as it is spelled in Captain Cook's voyages. From here I make as straight a track as I can for the Line and right North, level with San Francisco. Then a straight line towards the American coast, following it down to San Diego. All I want is wind and plenty of it, for the Ladas is getting sluggish in light winds. Goodnight, from your Father,   *T.M.*

June 4th.
Calm clear moonlit weather. The ship is rolling gently from side to side, with a long swell in the ocean, with the surface as smooth as glass almost. We only made 56 miles in the last 24 hours and evidently are not going to do so much the next 24. That is bad work indeed, but I can't help it, only toil on as fast as we can.

Saturday Night, 8th June.
Still calm weather, a beautifully clear sky. Have taken 5 days to do one day's work; only 33 miles today. A big ugly brute of a shark was around the ship this forenoon. So we put a hook and 4 pounds of pork on it over the stern and he grabbed it at once. But on passing the line along to the middle of the ship, it became slack and the hook came out. For a minute or two the shark did not seem to know he was free. But when he did realise the fact, the way that fish went for deep water was something to see. For the water here is so clean, we can see far away down many a fathom. I should think he took a bad toothache away with him; at any rate he did not come back for any more pork.

Our time is getting on. We are now 21 days from Port and a long way from the Line yet. Hope we will soon get a start now, as a gentle breeze is coming up and may increase. The weather is getting far too hot now for anything. Wish I could go up onto the Blue Mountains to see Mrs K. and family and get myself cooled down a bit. As it is, I get from the bed to the sofa, then back again, looking for the coolest place. In the day time, several flies about will not be chased out of the cabin, but dodge around and will insist on alighting on my nose the moment I am seated.

We passed a little low island the other morning called Palmerston Island. There are five of them in a cluster and we must have been very close to them.

Sunday 16th June.
For the last few days we have been doing fairly well through the

Trades and crossed the Equator yesterday 28 days out, having run over 2200 miles from Newcastle. So we should get to San Diego inside of 70 days. I hope to be not much over 60, but it all depends on the winds we get. We are getting towards the finish of the SE Trades now and they are getting squally and showery, but still a fresh breeze and I hope they will carry us into the NE Trades without delay.

You will now soon be getting your holiday from school and where are you going to spend them I wonder. Not with your poor old father here, sailing across the Pacific Ocean; but I believe you would like to be here with me and I hope some day you may be. God be with you till we meet again.

Sunday 23rd June.
Proceeding slowly on our way, lovely weather, gentle NE Trades and smooth sea. The ship glides along 6 miles an hour and makes no noise about it. We will likely see the French Frigate Island tomorrow if the wind stays the same. We have had a few boobys and man of war birds about today and a number of flying fish. Have never crossed the tropics and seen so few fish before. Nothing but a few flying fish since we had the shark on the pork and lost it. We have still nearly 3000 miles to go to reach our Port and I hope we may have a good wind to do it with. Another 2 or 3 days more will carry us outside the limits of these Trades, to 28 or 30 degrees North and into variable weather. Not too fine I hope.

June 25th 1895.
The French Frigate Island has been rather an unfortunate position for us. For we have been becalmed since noon Saturday; the sea very smooth with little appearance of wind around, only a few screeching sea birds about. This morning they had another shark on the hook and nearly had him on board, but he slipped off again and had business in deeper water. But this afternoon at 4 o'clock they got a big ugly one on board, about 9 feet long, with a mouth on him big enough to take a man's head. When sailors get a shark on deck they always want to know what he had for dinner last. They cut him up into bits, preserve his backbone for a walking stick,

his jaws for curiosity and stick his head on the boom end at the end of the ship. Well this one had in him nothing but a stick about two feet long they had used for stirring paint and had thrown overboard this forenoon. So no wonder he was hungry and went for the pork in a hurry as soon as it touched the water. As we are right under the sun now, it is very hot, with no wind about to cool it.

26th June, Evening.
Have got a cool breeze now and will get away North a bit; hope to have no more calms. Today we had two Cape hens about. They are a big black bird and only seen in the Southern Ocean. So they are a long way from home. I tried to catch one with a hook but coud not do so. They were very hungry and went after anything thrown overboard, but seemed to know the hook. It is quite refreshing to hear the water rippling past the ship again.
Sunday 30th.
Still carrying a nice little breeze along with us. We are not getting nearer to our Port. In fact we are getting a little further away; but we must go on North out of this wind to get a fair one, if there are any about.

We are now 43 days out; more days are passing and we are not getting any nearer our destination, with 2500 miles to go yet. No chance of getting there in 60 days now and will do fairly well if we are there in 70. Well I will try not to get too anxious about it but get on as fast as I can. If you look at the map of the North Pacific Ocean you will see we are nearly in the middle of it, between San Francisco one side and Japan on the other, just North of the Sandwich Islands.

We are getting cooler weather again now but as it is Summer time, the sun is very hot in the day time and it will be very hot in San Diego. That is if we are not too long in getting there. The Ladas is all painted up ready for Port now and only wants a 14 days good wind to get there.

Tuesday July 2nd.
Two days calms and light head wind and not a mile nearer to our Port. It looks as calm as it possibly can at present. I almost wish I had not known we had to get to Victoria by the 1st of Septem-

ber; then I would not have been so very anxious about a day or two's calm. But if we have much more of it, I am afraid it will make an old man of me. I get so surly and angry and mad enough for anything, laying here just like 'a painted ship upon a painted ocean'. Well we may get some wind tomorrow, so I will hope on for the time being and try to believe that God in His own time will send a breeze to get me into Port. So Goodnight.

Wednesday 3rd July.
Caught a shark today, a blue one about 8 feet long and found no less than 48 young ones in it. So we rid the ocean of 49 sharks at one sweep. Another one was around but it would not bite. The birds sitting on the water took no notice of it, although I saw it rub against one with its fin.

Thursday 4th.
A gentle breeze all day and for the first time this voyage we had dolphins about, but they could not catch any. Dolphins are not often seen so far North; they usually keep among the flying fishes. The birds have not been able to keep up with the ship today, swimming alongside as they did yesterday, waiting for anything thrown over from the galley. They will only eat fat meat, will not touch biscuit and did not seem to eat the pieces of shark thrown overboard.

Friday 10pm.
Glorious breeze going 10 knots. Something fresh to see the ship booming through the water again. Now I want her to go faster still. But long may the breeze last for the present; 10 days will do us to San Diego and the winds say 'Wouldn't you like to get it'.

Sunday Night.
Dear Mary Adelaide, it will now be Monday morning and you will be preparing for school if everything is all right with you and your holidays are over. Well we are going on our way with a nice little fair wind; not very fast but I must be thankful for small mercies. Our good breeze the other night dropped very suddenly at daylight and left us with a light wind and heavy rain all day. Today it

has been very fine and clear with a pleasant breeze. It is just cold enough to wear a jacket and need a couple of blankets at night now. I hope I shall not be over a fortnight before I get into Port and have your letters to read. Also perhaps a reprimanding from Mr Ritson for going the way I did to Newcastle, thus not getting to San Diego fast enough. The boys are just heaving the log to see how fast the ship is going and their clumsy feet made a horrible row overhead. Three of the boys are growing quite big lads but the little one is not any bigger. They say he orders the others about in the house and calls them names. So Goodnight.

12th July.
Dear Daughter, I must just talk a little to you to see if it will put me in any better humour. For these persistent head winds, light winds and no wind at all are making me very cross indeed. For 3 days now I have done almost nothing in the way of getting nearer my Port, in spite of all my best endeavours. No other point of the compass will do for the wind but right ahead. Still we have 1400 miles to go and it looks as if we are going to be a month doing it. There; a little grumble has eased my mind a bit and I hope it will not annoy you.

We have only seen one vessel since we left Port, but in a few days will likely see some more going into San Francisco, if we get a breeze to put us nearer the land. It is tantalising for fog and rain; just as we think it is going to be fair, along comes another shower and only a very little wind. There are still a few birds about but that is all. The weather is just warm enough and just cold enough now for me, the thermometer being at 65 degrees, but you don't know that instrument yet.

I have got the ships photograph framed, also several I got from Mrs Knight and intend to decorate my room with them. So it will look quite gay, with the big picture of the ship up as well.

Sunday 14th July.
We still have light head wind and often calm, so we get no nearer our Port. In fact I am trying to get away North to find some wind but, the breeze being so light and fitful, we can not get any where. However I am persuading myself that it is no use fretting about not having a steam boat under my feet. I must just wait

patient until I do get a fair wind. I am just tired and longing to get to Port now for a change of diet; our potatoes are nearly all done and when they are done, we have no other substitute for them but rice. Another fortnight yet for us at sea.

Sunday 21st July.
Well I have spent this last week doing very little and today I am just doing the same as I was last Sunday, with a very faint head wind. I am trying to get North again. The breeze has been right ahead from the same place all the week and I can not see any sign of a change yet. As we are very little nearer than we were last Sunday, we may very likely be 3 weeks longer yet. I hope not, or it will be a very long passage for us and Mr. Ritson will be mad.

Saturday 27th July.
We have a had a little fair wind today, the first for 18 days. For the last 3 days we have had ship in company called the Penthesilia of Liverpool from Panama for San Francisco, 51 days out, making as bad work of it as we are. He had only half the distance to come. We sailed past him once, but she came up again today with a breeze, but she is away behind us again now.

We had a very big shark around the ship yesterday. He seemed to be biting at the grass along the ship's side, but would not have anything to do with the pork we offered it. The birds seem all to have left us today; for the last fortnight they have been watching for everything that went over the side. When calm they swim alongside, abreast of the galley door, waiting for a chance piece of fat meat. They have become very cunning and very tame, so we have missed them today. I suppose they are giving the ships a turn.

We have a little fair wind at present, but not a very decided one. It must be a change for good though, as I am all full of aches and pains and generally in a very old and rheumatic condition. I see we have only made 80 miles nearer San Diego since last Sunday. We have still a 1000 miles to go and as we are over 70 days out, it looks as if we will not be far short of 90 before we get there. The weather has been so dry for the last week and the decks have dried up, so that I was nearly washed out of my room this afternoon by the water running through. But I have stopped it, all but one place in the bath room.

Friday August 2nd, 9pm.
We are travelling along in good style once again, going along at 10 knots an hour and would soon pitch into Port at this rate. But it has been too long in coming to save our passage. I can not lessen the 80 days, so a day or two more or a week matter little now. Still I am letting her go for all she is worth to get in as soon as possible. Hope I may get in on Tuesday at any rate; it is quite fresh to feel her going once more.

August 9th 1895.
At last I am safe in Port, after a passage of 81 days. Should not be very long in here, perhaps 3 weeks. They will not start discharging until next week.

I notice Aunt H. and you have been to the Lake District for your holidays and I hope you put in a pretty good time there, but not to wear out all your new frocks. Because you see if the Ladas does not make good time coming home from Victoria, I will not have any money to buy you more. I am going from here to Victoria (Vancouver) to load salmon tins in cases, for either London or Liverpool. I won't know until we are loaded.

San Diego is a very nice little city of 20,000 inhabitants, with very nice electric tramcars running around in it in a circular track. It is chiefly noted as having the largest hotel in the world, just outside across the Bay, capable of holding 1000 people, occupying 7 acres of ground. I have not been to see it yet but intend to do so some day soon.

I had a letter from Mrs O'Neill that Aunt H. sent me out. She tells me that this baby she has now is not as quiet as the one that died and she sends her kind love to you.

Some of the boys have got the report cut out of the Maryport paper. I suppose someone sent the paper home from Australia and they have copied it. I think you could not have got my last letters from Corral, as Aunt H. does not say she gets the money from the Owners that I asked them to let her have, or not.

So Miss Temple is going to get married then. Who will take her place there, Miss Richardson? I have not got any home papers from anyone; only Charlie sends me a London paper and writes me a long letter that his wife is waiting for a parrot he asked me to get in Newcastle for her. I did not do so and will have to send an excuse from here. He complains H. has not sent him our portraits yet.

Now I am here, I am eager to get out of this and get up to the loading Port. But I must wait my time.

With kind love to you and best regards to Grandparents, I remain Your Father,   *T. Messenger*

Write to; Barque Ladas, Victoria, British Columbia.

I suppose you will get this in 14 days or so.

SAN DIEGO TO VICTORIA, 1895.

Barque Ladas, San Diego,   *August 18th, 1895.*

My Dear Daughter,
They have not started to discharge our cargo yet, but will do so tomorrow and next day, so they say. They have had no room on their bunkers for our cargo up to the present, but think they will be able to clear some away next week. The bunkers hold 50,000 tons of coal and some very large ships have been here lately and filled it up.

There is a rowing club of young girls here and they have a splendid 8-oared gig which cost them 60 dollars; it is very elaborately fitted up. They came alongside and all of them came aboard today, dressed in their rowing costume; a blue sailor frock, with yellow lace on their collars and caps. They were very pleased with the Ladas and had a good look round. There are other clubs of lady rowers here, but these were the Champions. They could row very well, but they soon want to rest and have a talk. The Captain of the boat is a school teacher and of course she has plenty of talk and an air of command about her which keeps the young ones in subjection. They all very much admire the wax flowers I brought from Corral.

We have been here now 10 days, laying doing nothing. But when they do start they can put my cargo out in 5 days and ballast in in one and a half. I see Mr Dawson's ship the Wythop is up in Victoria yet; likely she is loading salmon too. I hope I shall be able to get away tomorrow week and get a good start out and up to the next Port.

I was looking for another letter from you here, but I suppose you think one is enough for me in this place. Letters can come here in a fortnight. All the ladies here ride bicycles, so when you learn to ride one I will buy you one. Perhaps I may try to learn here myself, then I can race Richard Tiffin, but not young Dick. I see he has been winning prizes at Maryport again.

It is Sunday night and all the crew are walking about, waiting for the Christian Endeavour people to come aboard and sing hymns with them. I have heard them practising all week, so we should have some good hymns tonight.

Trusting that you are quite well and enjoying yourself, I remain your loving Father,   *T. Messenger.*

Write to; Barque Ladas, Victoria, Vancouver Island, British Columbia.

(They are coming singing as they come in their boats and it all sounds nice on the water. Kind regards to your Grandparents and Aunt Hannah. Mind you write soon.)

Barque Ladas.   *San Diego, Sunday Night, August 25th, 1895*

My Dear Daughter,
I have just been listening to the people singing on board another vessel that has taken up our berth and it sounds well over the water. They have just been singing 'In the book of thy Kingdom, is my name written there and the mistakes of my life have been many'. There is no person but what could sing that with truth and feeling.

I thought to have been ready for sea by now, but I am much afraid that I will not get away this next week, as they can't get cars to take away the coals. They only worked two days and a half and put out 1350 tons, so we still have 800 tons in and they can easy finish that in two days when they have room. But when that will be, nobody knows.

I hear some of the sailors drunk on deck, so they have not been able to keep the pledge long. I believe they did manage to keep it for two nights after we got alongside. It is only the old men who are drunkards.

Everybody wants to know what we think of the climate here and they impress upon us what a fine country it is. And so it is, only too much the same all the year round, never very hot nor very cold in winter, only sometimes rainy then. Lots of people want to buy these wax flowers off me, but I tell them no; I am going to take them home. Their favourite expression is, 'Oh, isn't that just cute,' or 'isn't that just sweet'. But I find the people are very sociable here

96

and I think all the crew have been having a very good time here.

All the people are just leaving the other Barque and singing They'll never say good-bye. As it is nearly ten o'clock, it is time they were going home. Now they are singing, 'God be with you till we meet again' as they are rowing to the shore and I echo the sentiment to you with all my heart. Trusting to meet you again in a few months more.

With love I remain your father, *T. Messenger.*

San Diego,   *August 29th, 1895.*

My Dear Daughter,
The chapel people have just been here and gone, after holding a farewell service on the deck with the crew and they presented everyone from the Captain down with a Ditto(sic) bag, containing needles, thread, pen, pencil, writing paper, scissors, thimble, a very small comb and case and a lump of beeswax sticking plaster, plus various other things useful and necessary. I am writing this now with their penholder and paper and I will enclose their fancy sticking plaster.

There were only a very few here tonight to what there was the first time they came and tonight they were mostly elderly ladies and sedate middle aged gentlemen. They got through their work in good time and a few of them only had time to look in the cabin. So you need not be alarmed and think that the ladies here are going to run away with your poor old father. They never even invited me to tea, only the sailors and boys. One of the men that ran away, I let him get a pair of new trousers to go to chapel and tea with and he cleared out with them. I hear he has gone up country to pick grapes and other fruit.

This is such a great fruit-growing country that all shopkeepers keep lots just standing outside their front doors for their customers to help themselves. I wish I could just send you a box of pears, peaches and grapes.

I have only a short passage this time before me; a month or 35 days I suppose it will take us. So you must write back aoon after you receive this and twice after a fornight each time and tell me how

97

you are getting on with your teaching and your own learning.

I told you before how they all ride bicycles here and wear bloomer costumes; very ugly things they are too. A great many ride in their ordinary skirts. I was talking to one of the young ladies of the rowing club and she invited me out to see where they are camped. They were going to have a dance. They have a tent and have camped out for a week but she said they would break camp soon. I had to beg to be excused, although she told me there was plenty of young ladies out there to dance with, a dozen or so and I must say she was a very handsome girl herself. If I could have danced and looked 20 years younger, I might have gone and had a good time with them. But alas for my departed youth, I had to beg to be excused on the plea of very pressing business.

Trusting you are all well at the lodge, I remain ever your affectionate Father,   *T. Messenger.*

Barque Ladas, 8 days from San Diego.   *Sunday Sept 8th 1895.*

My dear Daughter,

I will make use of some paper the good folks of San Diego gave me to write to you again. It is a whole 8 days since we sailed and I suppose we are about half way to Victoria, though actually not any nearer in distance than if I had been at San Diego yet. But I had to make a big circle to get here on account of the wind being right against us this time of the year. If I can only make the other half of the passage in the same time, I will have done very well indeed, though I have no expectations of doing so. A good few of my men are troubled with bad colds in the head and choked up with coal dust. The nights have been very cold since we left; it is quite a change of warm weather today, though it has put the wind right ahead of us. However I must not grumble yet this passage. Everybody that had been to Victoria in San Diego praised it up for a very fine little town and so thoroughly English. I think it will be about the size of Maryport and they say everybody is in bed by about 9 o'clock, because there is no-one on the streets to be seen. However I will be able to tell you all about that when I get there and see the place for myself. Last voyage in the Dunboyne, we passed close by it going to Vancouver City.

Sunday Sept 15th.
At noon today, we are only 260 miles from the entrance to the Straits of Victoria. We have had a blustery, boisterous week of it this week, always getting a little nearer each day. Now I am afraid it should get too hazy for one to see anything and so not be able to find the Straits. But I trust that it will not be so and that I may get a run right in there, day after tomorrow; that would be a very good passage for the time of year.

I suppose Aunt H. and you got home safe from Mr Ellwood's and enjoyed yourselves while you were there. I hope you do not think I forgot your birthday, as I did not and went into a shop to get a card for you but the young lady was busy and I could not wait just then, so I told her I would call again but forgot to do so. Possibly she is waiting yet for me to call again, but it won't be this voyage.

It is a doubtful, dubious night; it may start in about midnight to blow very hard, as it has done one or two nights this week.

Wednesday Night, 18th.
Dear Mary, I am here in Royal Roads, anchored after a passage of 18 days, very good for the time of the year. I was in calm outside here all day yesterday and had to take a steamer to tow me up here. Victoria is about 3 miles from this; I went there today and got my letters, 1 from Australia and two from Mr Ritson, but none from Mary Adelaide. Is she very busy teaching, do you know and can't write a line or two to her father? Well no matter, one will come along bye and bye I hope. We are like to be here about six weeks, so they say, so you will have lots of time to answer this before I leave. Victoria is a very pretty place and the place right opposite here, Esquimault Bay, is a lovely spot. A Man of War lay in it and there is a Government Dock there for them.

With kind love, I remain your Father, *T. Messenger.*

Barque 'Ladas'.   *Victoria B.C.*   *Monday, Oct.7th 95.*

My Dear Daughter,
I have been looking long for a letter from you as I have had answers to my last letter from Mr Ritson (last letter from San Diego I mean).

But with the exception of your Aunt Lizzie at Crosby, I have had none from home here and I am now nearly three weeks here. I have been on the Marine Railway and had the ship cleaned and painted and should make a good passage home now. I have not got much cargo in yet, but there is some more ready for us to take in tomorrow. However I am afraid it will be into next month before we get away from here, they have so far to bring the cargo.

Victoria is a very nice little town and seems very brisk. I see there are a good many Cumberland people here, but none that I know, so I have not made any acquaintances yet. Where we lay is about three-quarters of a mile from the town, but the electric cars run down close to, on account of so many steamboats calling here from China, from San Francisco and from Alaska - that is the country away to the North of British Columbia.

Yesterday a man sitting on the end of the pier fell off but fortunately a boat was at hand and picked him up. I think he must have been drunk, he had only one arm. He never said a word when they put him in the boat and went to some steps and two men walked him off home.

It is getting cold weather now at nights and is very foggy and damp, so I got a very bad cold a week ago but have got nicely clear of it now. I got some honey in San Diego, thinking I could make something by selling it up here, but they do not care to buy it as they have a Duty of one and a half pence a pound to pay for landing it here, so I may have to take it right home with me.

I suppose you have been having more holidays, if the schools have been closed for sickness, as I think Aunt Lizzie said they had. I have had several letters and many papers from Australia; they are all well there, all got work and all hoping for the Ladas to go to Sydney next voyage. But it will be some time before we finish this one yet.

I have not lost any of my crew to run away here yet and it is not likely they will do so now, unless the new man I got in San Diego should do so, as he has no money to lose. But I don't think he will, he had enough of San Diego, running away from his other ship.

I hope your Grandfather and Mother are quite well and also your Aunt Hanna Menhams. Trusting soon to have a letter from you,

I am still your loving father,   *T. Messenger.*

Barque Ladas, Victoria, B.C.   *Tues., October 29th, 1895.*

My Dear Daughter,
Your long expected letter came at last and I am sorry you had not time to write before. However I am very glad to see you are all well and was pleased with the picture of you all, though at first I could hardly make out who you all were. You have been staring too hard and unless you have much altered since I last saw you; it is anything but good of you.

Well I will be loaded by tomorrow night or next morning and hope to sail on Thursday night from here. Then I will be out of the Straits by daylight in the morning. But it is so foggy that one can not see any distance. The bells are ringing and foghorns blowing more or less all the time. There will be several ships all leaving here all more or less about the same time, so the Ladas will have a chance of seeing if her clean bottom will benefit her.

Mr Ritson's ship the Auchencairn will probably be leaving Portland here about the same time. The Ladas is going to take a bigger cargo than I expected, probably about 63,000 cases, valued at as many pounds. So you see, salmon is a very valuable cargo. It is getting quite Wintery at nights here but the days are still warm when the sun shines through. These fogs make it very cold.

I had a letter from R. Ferguson and he says Aunt Mary is home and not very well, but is going back to London again when she gets better.

Well, you will not have a chance to see London this time, but will have to be content with Liverpool for a change. So you had better get your Aunt to fix you up with a trip. I suppose your Uncle James is still in Liverpool. I wonder if Mr Richmond sold Moor Park. I ought to have been at home and bid for it, but I am always away when bargains are to be had. Besides, I will have to make some more money with the Ladas first. Everybody thinks her a very fine ship here and they seldom have had one to take such a cargo of salmon away from this Port. I know Mr Ritson will be looking every day for a cable gram to say I have sailed.

With best love to you and kind regards to Grandfather and mother, I am your loving Father,

T. Messenger.

VICTORIA TO LIVERPOOL, 1895/6.

Barque Ladas,   *At Sea, Lat. 32 30 N, Long. 127 30 W.*

My Dear Daughter,
We are now nine days sailed from Victoria and have had fairly good progress so far for the time of the year, coming down the coast. But we have made most of the distance the last two days, with a fine fair wind which is just now dying out; or rather the ship is running out of it.

The ship having been cleaned and painted in dock sails very well now and I hope we will make a good passage home. But it is a bad time of the year in the Atlantic Oceans, North and South.

I have taken a notion to cut all my whiskers off and shave clean. I am surprised at the difference in myself, no improvement I am sure. You would not know your father if you saw me now. I think the man at the wheel thought I was a stowaway today when I came up out of the cabin. The little dog the boys have got looked at me for a stranger.

So far the Ladas has left all the ships behind that left the Straits with us and I trust we shall see no more of them this passage.

Sunday, Nov 11th.

Dear Mary,
As I look at the photo Hannah sent me of you, I am thinking that you will now be about to get up, as it is half past seven on Monday morning with you. That is eight hours difference to us here, half past eleven. So you see I am sitting up late writing this, though I never go to bed before this time now. When I can sleep when I like I get up when I like, but I am always out before 8 o'clock.

We have made a very fair run so far on our way, but now our wind is very faint indeed and what is worse it looks very calm all round. I hope it will not last long. You will likely know that I am on my way home by this time and will be looking forward to my arrival. But it is a very long way to Liverpool and a long while to look forward to the beginning or probably the middle of March. However please God, I hope we shall arrive all in good time.

Sunday November 24th.
We have not made such very good progress this last week, having had very slight and variable winds. But today we seem to have got the SE Trade winds; very light at present but will probably soon increase, or I hope so. Unless it does, our passage will be spoiled. I am now 24 days out and still 500 miles from the Equator and will probably take 5 days more to reach there. But if it keeps calm I may be 10 instead and that would be a long passage. If I get across in 25 days, I will be satisfied, giving myself 35 more to the Horn and 65 more from there to Liverpool. That would be a very fair passage home.

Everything jogs on on board this fine, dreamy kind of weather. There have been very few fish about. One night there were quite a lot of flying fish, two very large ones amongst them. Some of the sailors have hung them up to cure them. I told them they were not a bit hungry or they would have eaten them instead. A flying fish is nearly as big as herring as a rule, but these two were nearly as big as a mackerel and would make a good breakfast for one man. I hear a few porpoises snorting about tonight and tumbling about over each other in their frolicsome, playful manner.

Now we are near the Equator and the men think their arms are six inches longer, with pulling the yards around so many times, trying first one way and then the other to get a mile or two further South. Yet we are 270 miles from the line. Though I believe we have the Trade wind, it is dead against us, so we can not make much way in the right direction. We have made just 240 miles since last Sunday and have had lots of rain most of the week.

I am just letting my whiskers grow again so that I may have them a good length when we get into the cold weather again. We are swarmed out with moths in the cabin here and the more we kill, the more seem to come. They have been harbouring in two bushes of mountain moss I got up in Katoomba. I was reading the account in the Maryport paper of the Crosby Bazaar and the stall holders, but you were not amongst them. No matter, there were plenty without you.

Sunday December 8th 1895.

Well we have been doing some very good work this week. We are well away down the SE Trades now and hope in a few days more to pass Pitcairn Island. We are only between 7-800 miles off it. It is a lonely Island, 2 and a half miles long by one mile wide. The inhabitants are all English speaking, being descendants of the Mutineers of the Bounty, a tale I think you will have read about in the school books. I have never sighted the island, as often as I have passed down here before. So I hope I may be able to see it this time and if possible call and give the natives any books I have to spare. American ships make a point of calling here and leaving papers for them when convenient.

Every morning after sunrise and every evening after sunset, we are treated to a very sharp squall and heavy shower. This morning at half past seven a hard squall came on and of course lay the ship over on her side. She took a dip forward into the sea, bringing a lot of water on deck. I saw one of the men lifted off his feet with the water, up to his waist. Of course now the weather is warm it was only a little bit of a plunge bath for him.

There is 10 o'clock just struck; that will be half past six for you at home. Now our days are getting longer every day and yours are at their shortest. I hope to be near Cape Horn by New Year's Day. We have a couple of birds keeping us company this last day or two; they are only gulls. In a week's time, we will be looking for Cape pigeons, albatross and Cape hens. The ship is laying over so much on her side that I have to sleep on the sofa. I can not keep in the bed; she is like to roll me out.

Sunday Dec. 15th.

This week we have not got on so very well, but might have been much worse, as we still keep on our way. On Wednesday last we passed a desolate looking island (Elizabeth Island). It is about 5 miles long, 80 feet high and very flat and level the full length of it. I could not help thinking it looked like the first ice we saw going to Newcastle. This morning the first albatross put in an appearance to let us know that we were approaching the stormy regions. The weather is still very hot in the daytime, though the air is cooler at night and I want some blankets to keep me warm. We have daylight now up to half past seven and days are getting longer every day as we go South. I should just like to run from here to Cape Horn in 14 days more, but I don't expect to do so and shall not complain if I get there in 20 days. I am striving not to be too impatient when the winds are light and nearly calm.

Sunday Dec. 22nd.
We have not made such very good progress this week, but could easily reach Cape Horn in 10 days time yet. Just today though the wind is partly against us and I hope it will shift more favourable very soon before I get South amongst ice again. We are getting now into cold weather and I have long days from half past three until half past eight. So far the weather is beautifully fine and sea smooth and we are crawling on our way home easily and steadily, though not swiftly by any means. There are no birds about to keep us company, only one old grey albatross and he does not come very near us.

A very few days more and we will have Christmas again and not so very far from where we had the last one (Corral). The weather is still fairly warm yet. But a couple of nights ago the boy Ross (the little fellow) likely found it chilly on deck, for they lost him. They hunted for half an hour all over the ship before they found him under the mess room table fast asleep. So next day in his watch below, I made the young rascal scrub it out, though I could not help smiling at his choice of place to lay down.

Christmas Day.
We are travelling along some today, with a strong fair wind and a big sea behind. Yesterday we ran 250 miles and if we continue as we are at present, we should do about 280 or therabouts by noon tomorrow. It is never very comfortable when we are going so fast; the ship tumbles about too much for that and fills the decks too much with water. But for the sake of getting on, we will put up with the discomfort. I am only afraid it is too good a breeze to last, but I am determined to make the most of it. So I am letting the Ladas go for all she is worth.

I trust you are enjoying a good time at home during this Festive season.

December 29th, Sunday.
The Ladas is still staggering and rolling on her way to the Cape and shapes fair for getting to it by New Year's Day. If she does I must not grumble at her, for that will make a fair run from Victoria. I only hope I may get on as well through the Atlantic Oceans and get to Liverpool in another 60 days from there; that would make a very good passage. It is a little over 10 months since I passed this way to Newcastle and what a circle I have sailed since then.

We keep looking out keenly for ice now, but have not seen any yet and hope we may not do so.

January 2nd, 1896.
We passed close by Cape Horn at 7 o'clock last night and at noon today were past Staten Island. The next we have to pass will be the Falkland Islands. Today we have two ships in company. A five-masted Barque signalled and she is the Lord Elgin from San Francisco, 60 days out same as myself. We were 8 days getting to Frisco, so we have done better than he so far. We spent New Year's Day passing close along the land and a fine day we had. We saw the Lion Rock of the Horn quite close. It is a rock with a lump on top, just like a lion crouching on it.

Sunday Jan. 5th 96.
Dear Mary, we are running along in fine style now towards home, having the ship's head pointing to the North. As we get along, our days are getting shorter, 3/4 of an hour shorter already. The Second Mate and some of the Maryport men thought we had passed the Wythop this morning, but I think it was a mistake. We passed some Barque like ourselves, but he was taking it easy, with a lot of his sails in. Or he may have had more wind yesterday than we had. We had a good hard breeze, skimming along at 11 or 12 miles an hour a good part of the time. The Ladas is making a flyer of herself, passing all the ships so rapidly. I only hope she may keep on at it all the way home and not get stopped anywhere with calms or head winds.

Now I am round the Horn properly and on my straight road home, I feel as if we were going to be there next week, instead of two months time yet. Of course we are getting into warmer weather every day now and are not likely to see any ice this time, but are not yet entirely clear of where it has been seen before.

Sunday 12th Jan.
Another week's journey nearer home and we have got into warmer weather again, having to take some of our clothes off. Tonight it is calm and a wet, dense fog, like rain. Quite a change after the last two days, as the ship was pitching bows under into a big head sea and kicking up a big dust or spray. We grumbled at that and now we grumble because it is too fine; so you see we are bad to please at sea as well as on shore.

Our troubles are only now about to commence, as this is the worst, or rather most tedious, part of the passage. To get from here up into the SE Trades; it is getting through this 1000 miles more or less that mostly spoils all passages. So far I have done very well in 70 days, but if I am baffled here for long, it will spoil it and my chance of getting home in 120 days.

We have passed quite a few vessels this week. On one day I passed between a German Barque from Chile to Hamburg, 47 days out and a French Barque from Chile, 35 days out. At the rate we passed them they must have thought the Ladas was a flyer. Another day I passed three, also very fast, but only one signalled. They call her the Aspice, from the Gulf of California for Cork, 84 days out. She seemed very slow, but the Ladas being clean made all the difference. If we had not been cleaned and painted in Victoria, we would have been slow too. Now we are becalmed, all the slow ships may come up to us again with a breeze. So Goodnight. X.

Sunday 19th Jan. 96.

My Dear Mary,
Another week nearer home and we have made pretty fair progress during this week. Still we have not got into the SE Trades yet. In fact the wind we now have is just opposite, but as it is favourable I don't mind it much.

We have had quite a time of it since 3 o'clock this morning. A very violent storm came on and threw the ship over on her side, so that the Port side was clean under water. The water went into the houses and came through the cabin door into the Mate's room, up to the saloon door. It was daylight before we could get sails off the ship and her upright and clear of water. But we did do so at last and a fine job they had then to clear all the ropes about decks; as they were washed about in all directions, in every hole conceivable. Afterwards at about 8 o'clock it blew a furious storm for about an hour and then dropped all at once to a light breeze, shifting to the NW. So we had to 'Ware Ship', that is put the ship's head the other way; then set all the sails again, which kept the men at work until noon.

We had a ship in company all the forenoon and until 4'o clock, when she dropped out of sight astern. At 4 o'clock a vessel was sighted ahead going the same way as ourselves and before 6 we passed close by her. She was an Italian called Glama of Porto; he is many a mile astern by now. I am very glad we came out of the storm with no loss; only the wash deck tub got washed over the side.

Sunday 26th January.
This is my birthday but I had forgotten it. We have had a very nice quiet week since last Sunday and very fine weather. Now we have very nice breeze, Trade Winds and I hope to cross the Equator in another 4 days. Then the last stage of our journey will commence. I stand a chance of making the passage in 125 days or less.

We are busy painting ship around inside and are not going to have enough oil to finish with, but will just have to make the best of it. The weather is very warm now and we feel that clothes are a nuisance. But even at sea we have some little modesty left and a little respect for the proprieties, whatever our private inclination may be.

During the storm last Sunday, the Mate thought one of the boys had been washed overboard. He was found with the Carpenter in the house with water washing about them, saying their prayers while others were working on deck. I hear they don't intend to come to sea any more. But I think they have forgotten it by this time and I think they have got all their clothes dry.

Sunday February 2nd.

We are now well across the Line, in 6 degrees North Latitude and I think we have got hold of the NE Trade Winds. At any rate we have had NE winds for two days now. So we are getting along fairly well and I hope will continue to do so. I have been trying to get a flying fish for my old friend Charlie at Lancaster. The Second Mate says one came on board last night but smashed its head in on one of the boats forward, making a mess on the new paint. So I am afraid Charlie will have to wait for another voyage, as there seem to be very few about. The Second Mate got a fine one in the Pacific but the rats have eaten it.

Our days are getting short now, dark soon after 6 o'clock. They will not get much shorter as they will be growing longer at home now and by the time we reach the Channel should be daylight until 6. We are looking for the North Star but it is not clear enough tonight, as it will still be near the horizon yet. You see when we once see it we feel we are getting nearer home, as we can watch it rise up higher and higher every night.

Another Sunday, February 9th.

And we are just finishing up with the NE Trades, or apparently so. The breeze has died away to almost a calm and what little there is is dead against us. So far we must not grumble, only if this wind should hold long in this quarter. We will be very near the Bermuda Island in a few days, on the track for America instead of Liverpool. Today we have been sailing through Gulf weed and the boys have been filling bottles of it to take home, as all boys do on their first voyage. It is a seaweed floating about in the ocean and it is not known exactly where it comes from but lots of little crabs are found amongst it.

We are 98 days out now and I wonder if Liverpool will be in sight this day three weeks. It chiefly depends on the next 10 degrees, our getting over them. A distance of 120 miles daily would do it easily for us but I suppose we shall not have the luck to do that. No matter, I shall see you soon and so Goodnight.

Sunday 16th.

A full weeks time lost, as we are not any nearer home today than last Sunday. Though we have sailed some 300 miles or so since, it has not been straight for home. Most of the week has been calm. Today we are doing a little good with a faint breeze. The ship is all ready now for going into dock but that will still be three weeks or more, as last week was no good to us. We are still passing through Gulf weed, though it is getting scarcer and we will soon lose it altogether; I don't care how soon.

The sun is very hot in the daytime but the nights are very cool now and the days are short; from 6 to 6 now is all the daylight. We have been having long days for so long now that we can't get used to the short ones in a hurry. I have just been wondering if the Wythop, Capt. Davison's ship, is getting on any better than us and if she is home yet. He sailed 20 days before us and if she beats us on the passage Mr Ritson will be annoyed perhaps. I think I made myself bad with the paint in the cabin, as I was bad last night and this forenoon but feel all right again now.

Sunday 23rd February 96.
We have made a little better work this week but will have to do better next one if we are to reach Liverpool by next Sunday. We will have to keep on just as we are at present, going 10 miles an hour and not ease up on it all the way. We have had a strong gale and a big sea the last 24 hours and it seems to be keeping up the same for another 24.

This forenoon the Ladas was throwing water all over the Poop. She filled my boots on the Poop and wetted me through giving me a Sunday shower bath. So long as she is travelling through the water I don't mind it a bit. The weather is still very warm, quite mild in fact, but it will soon change if the wind gets in the North and we may have some March winds before we are home yet.

I think the men have all got their bags packed and labels ready for their chests and I daresay will have settled what train they will go by already. So if we are long in getting in from here, they will be very much disappointed. It is raining hard on deck and below the water is dripping all around my room, over the drawers and bed. It is stopping a little, so the deck will tighten up soon I hope.

I presume Mr. Ritson will be on the look out every day now for me but they will have to wait another 10 days I am afraid before I can report the Ladas off Holyhead.

Sunday March 1st.

A blustery windy day but a fair wind and we are getting nearer home every hour, still 600 miles off yet. The breeze last Sunday dropped and shifted ahead soon as I finished writing. In fact I left to go on deck, as I felt the wind on the other side and it came from the opposite direction and we only got along poorly all the week. The Ladas has been laying over on her side and tumbling things about today and is still doing so, though not so bad as she was.

Well next Sunday I will surely be in Liverpool; I hope to before that. At least we are making a good shape at present, if not served the same as last Sunday night. I will have to lay on the sofa tonight, or I will tumble out of bed the way the ship lies over.

Wednesday 4th March 1896.

Docked at last, after a good run in up Channel. Things seem so quiet and still here in dock, the ship being still. I am too tired and sleepy to write more tonight.

BARQUE MIDAS:
U.K. TO VALPARAISO, 1896.

Barque 'Midas',   *Tuesday Night, April 14th 1896.*

Dear Daughter,

I am now fairly well on my way and will be letting the tug go in an hour or two. You will be going back to your Grandma's likely. I have left the decision to yourself if you care to go on teaching and go to church and Sunday school, as they will likely expect you to when you are bound as a pupil teacher. After being at it for a year or two, if you then do not care for it, or it does not agree with you, you can give it up.

The wind is fair for us and I hope we may have a good run out of Channel when the steam tug leaves us. I find I have left my parallel rules on the mantel shelf at Birkby Moor, so I must do without them the best way I can.

I hope you all got up home dry, as it has been fair with us ever since we left dock. We are now nearly past the Isle of Man and will soon see the Skerries and then Holyhead.

When you go to Cockermouth, you must thank Maggie for her loaf. I forgot if it was for Willie or me. At any rate, I have been trying it and it is very good. It seems to have a small notion of raining now, but I hope it will keep off.

As I want just a little rest for an hour, while the tug boat has hold of us, I will close with kind love to yourself and Grandparents, also Aunt H. Menhams.

I remain your father, *T. Messenger,* Barque Midas, Lyons to Valparaiso, Chile.

(Write 50 days from now and it will be out there as soon as I will)

Barque Midas, Lat 48 N, Long 8 W.   *Sunday April 1896.*

My Dear Daughter,

You will now be back at Grandma's and your other Aunt H. will have your company to herself more now. Well turn about is fair play.

This is our first Sunday out and we have not made such good progress as I had hoped for. Still, it is better than I did in the Ladas and as I have a very nice little fair wind at present, I must not grumble. I think Willie has got over his sickness; he looks very thin and white in the face now after it. But we have not had any bad weather as yet to try them, the boys I mean. Neither have I had any wind to try how fast the Midas can sail, but I can see she can't sail with the Ladas by a good bit. I haven't yet found out the best place to put things and all my bundles are kicking around everywhere in the bathroom yet.

A very strange bird flew aboard yesterday and a comical look it has; it seems all neck and legs. It stands very upright and when anything attracts it, it stretches its neck out a great length like a miniature giraffe. It also has a very long sharp beak and may possibly be some sort of a woodpecker.

Sunday 26th April.

2nd Sunday out and we have made a bit more distance this week, having had a fair wind so far and now should be into the NE trade wind. I fancy we have got them already. At any rate we have got a North East wind and have had it all the week nearly. Last voyage I was 5 days longer getting to this place and I hope I may keep on gaining time all the way. We were just abreast of Madeira at noon today and about 100 miles off it, fairly well for twelve days time. If I can only get to the Equator in 12 more, we shall do well. I think that the boys are all clear of their sickness now and full fledged sailors. The Mate tells me that Willie does not like sea now and vows he will not come back again, but he will probably change his mind before he gets back home. The cabin floors are only now beginning to look a little decent, all the dirt getting washed off them now. We do not fall in with many ships at any rate. The only two we have seen, we have passed and so consider the Midas can go a little when she passes ships so well. One Barque was like the Dutch Barque Van Galen that was in the dock astern of the Ladas, but it was not her.

Tuesday night, April 28th.
We are now just 14 days out and a little past the Canary Islands - but instead of canaries, we have swallows paying us a visit, as we keep rolling along on course, with a very pleasant NE trade wind. I am sure you would be very much amused if you could see me sitting in my chair here these two nights, mending my clothes, letting unmentionables out and sewing on buttons. I conclude I must be getting stouter. Sitting at my table in the saloon yesterday, I happened to look at the glass and was amused to see a repetition of shiny heads nodding and smiling (ill-natured people might call it grinning) at me. I counted them as they appeared further and further away and less and less distinct. You see, the reflection from one glass to the other kept repeating the likeness without end. We are now 8 days ahead of our time to this position last voyage.

Sunday May 3rd.
Just abreast of the island of San Antonio this afternoon. It is very high; could only see the tops of the mountains this afternoon, the highest being 7100 feet. I suppose we were 20-15 miles off it. Our Trade winds keep very light so we have not gained any more time on last voyage and it is evident that I am not going to cross the Equator in less than 30 days from home. A large ship has been in sight all day, but she does not seem able to overtake. I have got hold of a very bad cold somewhere and can hardly hold my head up and it almost requires a towel to mop up all the water which runs from my nose and eyes. The weather is very warm now, as we are right under the sun, or will pass under it tomorrow. Still, it cools in the evenings a good deal and just suits me, this sort of weather. I am dreading the cold we will have off the Horn, the dead of Winter down there. I'm thinking Willie will not like it either.

Monday 4th
Ship Queen of England signalled, 2071 tons, of Liverpool.

Sunday May 10th.
How the days do run into weeks and the weeks into a month is surprising. Two days more and we will be a month out and by that time across the Equator, as we were just 200 miles off it at

noon today. So far we have had a very favourable passage and a very easy one, just gliding along through the water quietly and smoothly. Last night was not a pleasant one though, for it rained steadily from 8 until 2 this morning, and at 1 0'clock, some lightning and thunder passed very near the ship. Every rattle of thunder seemed as if it struck the ships side, it was so metallic, something like enormous pots and pans clanging together, causing the ship to shake all over. There was only a gentle breeze all the time. The weather cleared up fine after and it has been fine all day.

Tonight, the sea is illuminated all round by phosphorus in the water; looks as if innumerable electric lights were being carried around by invisible means. The ships wake is simply a line of lights behind her. It seems to me we have got hold of the SE trade winds; I hope it may prove so. A steamer from Victoria passed us on Tuesday, I wonder if he will report us. It is strange, we have had no vessels in sight for a few days now. It is very warm weather now and I change my bed place two or three times a night; first the chart house, then the bed, then the sofa. Last night, the thunder shook the chart house so that I had to leave it.

Sunday May 17th 1896.
Here we are getting along down the SE trades in good style. Yesterday we passed an Italian Barque bound for Montevideo, 52 days out and we were 32 out only. In another week or fortnight, we will be into cold weather and short days and then our troubles will begin, with our fight to get round Cape Horn. Hope we may be favoured and get round soon and make a good passage out for our first one, not more than 70 days. We could very easily do it in less. I see Mary that all the glass beads you put round this likeness are breaking off one by one. Perhaps if I get the Carpenter to make a stand for it, it may save them. This last few days, I see plenty of flying fish around but never a one comes on board. So I can not get one for Mr Charlie Anderson of the Folly Inn yet. I have an idea that Willie is not so much in love with the sea as he was. All the boys are getting to be useful now, but their troubles are before them yet; we have had nothing but lovely weather ever since we left.

Monday May 18th.
, Just after midnight last night it came on a heavy squall and rainy
and a very disagreeable head sea; the ship putting her bow right
under and then bringing her stern down with a flop heavy enough
to make things rattle about the cabin. I fancy some of the youngsters
would be sea sick as they have not had such a shaking up before.
If the wind had only been a little more favourable, they would have
had even more of a shaking, as I would have let the Midas go for all
she is worth, with all canvas on, instead of taking some off to ease
her into the sea.

Thursday May 21st 1896.
The wind has been unfavourable the last few days and has put us
on the coast of Brazil again, same as we were in the Ladas, but much
further South. Today we have had a strong breeze, squalls and rain;
the ship splashing water in all directions. A large Spanish steamer
passed us this afternoon and hoisted up his longitude. He likely
thought I was heading the ship into danger if I did not know my
position well. We are going right in to some shoals and small islets
called 'Abrothos' or 'Open your eyes' in English, so I intend to do
so. The light which is placed on one of the isles is visible 20 miles
and as it is a fine clear night, I hope to see it the full distance and not
stick the Midas on a rock.

   The weather is getting a bit cooler now and the days shorter and
it will be some time with us before they get any longer.

Sunday May 24th.
We have got on some distance this last three days and have got a
nice pleasant favourable wind pushing us along towards Cape
Horn. I see we are just as long from the Equator this time as we were
last and I hope we may not be any longer the rest of the way.

   I am wondering whether Mr Marsh has been for you to go to
Sunday School or not and if so how you like it. I have just wound
the saloon clock and it is 11 o'clock and English time it is still 3 hours
better, so you will be fast asleep at home now and perhaps dreaming. Well I sit in my chair with my feet up on the desk and do a good
deal of dreaming myself, hoping to have a fair weather passage
round the Cape. My crew are all young and will not be able to

manage the ship well in bad weather, so many not having been to sea before and the nights will be cold and long. I suppose we will get along through somehow, no use meeting troubles that never come. So Goodnight.

Sunday May 31st.
Well we had some little excitement this week. Caught suddenly by a hard gale Wednesday at noon and damaged some sails. The ship also filled the decks with water and the boy's house, wetting all the clothes in their chests. But as the weather was warm, no on cared much about getting wet. The ship has just given them a warning what to expect and to be careful to keep their doors shut in future. It has only been a kind of half and half weather since and tonight it is raining all the time, but only a light wind so we are not getting on very fast. But we are very little behind last voyage from the Equator yet.

Sunday night, June 7th.
A wild stormy night, but better than the last two. This is the third days hard gale and given us lots of work, carrying away our sails. Lots of damage to repair once it gets fine, whenever that may be. Willie is not in love with the sea now. The other boys are sticking to it manfully, all of them. I am almost giving up heart myself after the loss of these sails through putting defective gear on board and the wind continuing so persistently ahead. I am just a little sick of it; the Mate being laid up with a lame knee, I have to be on deck to see to everything myself. The weather is warmer than I expected down South here, but it may be cold enough at the Horn.

Sunday June 14th 1896
This has been a more disastrous week for sails and rigging than ever. In one gale, we did over £100 worth of damage; sails blown away entirely, or only ribbons left. Today is the finest day we have had for some time and I have replaced my sails by others, but some I can not replace as I have no others so must jog on as best we can without them.

For the last 9 days, we have only succeeded in making 180 miles in a direct way; been sailing round in a circle with furious storms most of the time. We are all very heartily tired of bad weather and welcome this relief of a fine day. Probably it may be fine for some little time now, at least I hope it will. I find lots of interesting bits in the Sunday paper you gave me. I wonder if you enjoy church Sunday School and the prospect of being tied to it for a few years. I suppose you will get used to it in time. We none of us like the things we are compelled to do, but stick to the things we know, rather than go looking for new things.   Goodnight.

Sunday June 21st 1896.

My Dear Mary,
We had a very narrow escape of shipwreck this morning at 4 o'clock, as we ran over the top of some sunken wreck. The ship made two thumps and scraped along over it. Fortunately the sea was very smooth and the land not so very far off; we could see some small islands, but we could not have landed on them had the ship been lost. However we got off all right and apparently no damage done, though I daresay the crew were all very much scared, as the man who was steering ran away from the wheel. You see I had a nice fair wind and was coming round the Falkland Islands, keeping close to the land in smooth water and got too close to the Sea Lion rocks lying to seaward of the Falklands..

It was just the commencement of ill-luck for us, as no sooner had we got clear, than it came on to blow and the wind went right ahead of us. Just as I thought we were having such a nice run along the land and away to Cape Horn, it has left me a sadly disappointed man, grumbling as only an old sailor knows how. I suffered with toothache and earache all last week and am hardly yet clear of it. The sailors were not long putting the life-boat in the tackles ready for launching. Fortunately she was not wanted, or I hope it is fortunate. Of course we might want it in a worse place and not be so well able to get it out.

A large 4-mast passed this afternoon, homeward-bound, swinging all his sails to the breeze and here are we jammed and under small canvas. No matter, our turn will come bye and bye. I trust we will have no more accidents this passage, I am getting tired of them. Four or five of the crew are little or no use now for pulling ropes. Their hands are all full of boils, so it makes work hard for the others.

Willie looks as if the cold would shrivel him up altogether. The other lads seem able to stand it very well and are getting very useful. But poor Willie looks thoroughly disappointed and disgusted with sea life. Of course, he has had a rather rough experience this last three weeks.

Sunday June 28th 1896.
Very little progress we have made this week, so I am a very much disgusted man still. The wind will only stop on the very worst point of the compass for us; then it blows too hard for us to do anything with it or there is too much sea on. The little bump we had does not seem to have done the ship any harm, so we can jog on with confidence yet. I put on the fire in the cabin this week and I can lie on the deck and look at it. It does not seem to warm the room up much. Still, it is something to look at these cold nights. I have to be on deck a good deal on account of both Mate and Bosun being laid up. I have to turn to and keep watch myself now, or at any rate be on deck when anything is being done. One of the boys fell on deck and cut his forehead and nose, so he came for some sticking plaster to put over it. I told him I would put a ticket on him as they did on cattle at Cockermouth Auction Mart and that next time he fell, he had to sit down and fall easy.

Monday July 6th 1896
The ship was kicking up such a lively racket all day yesterday that I could not sit at the desk to do any writing. A fierce gale set in at midnight the night before and caught us on a lee shore, so we had to turn about and come back South again. Such a terrific sea got up in a short time that the good ship Midas was tossed about anyhow and took so much water on deck there was just no getting along. The Steward got washed down and lost the breakfast coming aft with it. The Cook was not able to Cook any dinner for water in the galley, so we had to eat cold preserved meat for a change; we could hardly sit still to eat it. The boys I hear went forward into the Forecastle and deserted their place altogether. The gale is still continuing but not near so violent as it was and the sea is much easier, so the ship is going along comparitively quiet. We have lost 30 miles of ground and although we are West of Cape Horn, we are

not yet round it, being still South and going more South all the time; the wind keeping just right from the direction we want to go. So I give up hopes of reaching Valparaiso inside 100 days now. No doubt Mr Ritson is looking for a telegram daily; but it is no use, I can only fight my way against these winds mile by mile and what we gain one day, lose another. Just 200 miles West and I could have gone along with the wind fair with this gale. There is still something to be thankful for; it might have been cold, frosty, snowy weather, instead of being very mild for this Winter time of the year. While you were at church yesterday, you could not know what a lively tossing about we were having off Cape Horn here. Now the hail is pattering on the deck, but it soon melts.

Sunday 12th July 1896.
This has been a little better day than last Sunday was. Still not a pleasant or fine day by any means, as it is blowing half a gale and some sea up too. Worse still, the wind is right ahead. Now we are round Cape Horn, the wind goes with us and keeps right ahead mostly all the time. Once in two or three days we get just a few hours sun and then it is calm nearly. So we continue fighting our way round, a struggle for every mile of ground. I want to go right North now and of course the wind must come from there. When it was a good wind for us, we could never get it from that quarter.

The Mate and Boatswain are still laid up and one man also. Some others have have bad hands, so what with head winds, bad weather and short hands, I am about sick of this passage. Still it might have been worse, as we might have had cold, frost and snowy weather, whereas we have had it tolerably mild, very mild in fact for a Winter passage. All the lads have stuck to it bravely and I daresay Willie thinks Cape Horn not such a bad place after all.

14th July 96.
At midnight, the boy Light was washed across the decks and struck his head on something. As soon as he was helped to his feet, he commenced to call out 'I'm hurt somewhere, I'm hurt somewhere'. So I got him down to my room and found there was a very nasty cut on his forehead and the blood all down his face. I had to take him in the bathroom and clean his face to find the cut, which I fixed up

for him with some Friar's Balsam; the boy stood it bravely.

Sunday 19th July 1896.
At last we have fair wind and have had it for more than 24 hours. Unfortunately I had no sails left that I could set, or scarcely any. Now I have got some canvas spread and the good ship Midas is moving forward once more. On the 16th and 17th, we had a most furious storm and rain and found ourselves near the land. On the 17th at 3 o'clock it cleared up and there was the land ahead of us, near at hand. So we had to turn the ship round and get off it as soon as possible; we call it 'Waring Ship'. So all hands were out pretty lively and we even had her round and she did not wash the men about much after all, but gave us work until midnight. By 4 o'clock in the morning it was nearly calm and the sea smooth. You would never have thought what a furious storm we had just 12 hours before. The men and lads were all frightened the ship would get ashore; they had been asking if they would be drowned. I have had to hurry the men along mostly all the time, but that evening they pulled as hard and moved as ever they did in there lives and did not look as anxiously to see if any water was coming over them. So we looked very draggled and delapidated all day yesterday, but are squared up a bit now and some damages repaired. I have had to repair my own damages also; all the buttons off my vest and old overcoat and as the ones I have sewn on are of various sizes and patterns, no doubt I look very Irish. I hear that the lads in the half deck are not particular about putting on each other's clothes; first one up picks up the driest clothes, while the owner looks for some other things to put on. Now I think we will have some finer weather for a day or two and get things dry a bit.

Sunday 26th July 96.
This is a fine day, much warmer than last Sunday was and people can get their clothes out today. We have got on our way some distance this week and, with a little breeze, would get to Port in two days. Not having all our sails, the ship does not get on so fast as she would otherwise. It is quite pleasant to get some fine weather and feel the sun again, after all the cold and damp we have had. I rejoice at it as well as the boys. Of course we must not 'Hollo' before we are

out of the wood, we are not in Port yet; I may have more bad weather before we are, although only 340 miles off now.

The sailors have bought nearly all the clothes I had to sell and yet there are always some with salt water boils on their wrists and arms, caused by wet clothes chafing them. The boys seem to have the least ailing them of any.

Sunday August 2nd 1896.
A most wretched day for rain, mist and fog and a breeze ahead. This evening at 7 o'clock, some heavy rain came on and some lightning was about. A very brilliant electric light shone on all the mast heads and on the Royal Yard Arm. First I was surprised to see stars shining overhead, when all around was nothing but blackness and gloom. But the long stream of light settled along one of the wire ropes aloft and I knew what it was. It is quite a long while since I saw it before but it often occurs in changeable weather with lightning about.

We have just been going backwards on the same line these last 4 days and more, too foggy to try and make the Port, more or less rainy all the time and light winds right ahead mostly. We are somewhere about 80 or 90 miles off yet and may possibly be in tomorrow if it clears up and keeps moderate. I hope after this rain and lightning to get a little clearer sky. I am sure you will all be getting quite anxious about our safety. Mr. Ritson will at any rate. But when they come to know what damages we have had to sails, rigging and hull, they will be mad, no doubt. The Midas has (as a result) got so slow, there is no moving her without half a gale. We are making the longest time from the Straits of Lemaire (that, if you look on the map, you will see is the channel between the Staten Island and Terra del Fuego) of any ship I have ever heard of; now 36 days and not in yet. It may easy be another week if these fogs and rainy weather and calms keep up.

I'm reading over your Mother's letters tonight; it seemed like having her talk to me again and if it were like yesterday since I received them in the various parts of the world I was in then.

The rain keeps pattering on the deck above my head but I feel by the motion of the ship that the wind is dying away, the only little fair wind for some days now. Well no matter, we will get into Port

122

soon and we are all well and want for nothing, so need not grumble. Though we had an accident the other evening which might have been a serious one. A man fell from aloft, some 30 or 40 feet on to the deck and how he yelled. I felt sure he was all but killed. However it turns out he is not much hurt, but frightened a good deal.

Trusting you are all well at home, I am your father,

T. Messenger.

Tuesday August 4th 1896.
Anchored at 3 o'clock today after a long passage of 112 days. Just had time to get on shore and get your letters and it was dark before I got to the ship. We had a little trouble to find the ship; it is two miles ashore from where we are lying.

I notice you are going in heavy for school books; I hope you make good use of them. I trust you got the song off all right and did not frighten the Inspector when you sang it.

I am very much surprised the ship had not been reported, as I signalled a number of steamers on the early part of the passage. I suppose I will be here for two months and a half, getting rid of our cargo and there seems to be nothing doing here on the coast at all.

With kind love to you, hoping this finds you and all the rest quite well, I remain your father,

T. Messenger.

Barque Midas, Valparaiso, Chile.   *Sunday evening, 16 Aug 1896.*

My Dear Daughter,
We are now in here nearly a fortnight and have done but little towards getting clear of our cargo. You see, Valparaiso Bay is a very open place and with certain winds, even if very light, a swell comes in and the launches can not come out for the cargo. Especially for rails, as they are so liable with the least roll, to slip overboard or capsize the launch. They tell me that next month they have a number of holidays; as things are at present, we need not be in any hurry. Freights are so low and so bad to get. The town or city of Valparaiso is built all on the side of a hill, or rather various hills, In

places they have lifts to take people up and down, something like a switchback railway, only these are worked by steam. I walked out to the park yesterday and when I came back to the lift, it was full, so instead of waiting I walked down the hill and rather liked it.

I have had Willie and all the boys at the Bethel ship to service this morning and the vessel was rolling a little, so the young ladies who sing and play the harmonium did not seem to like it much. One of them sang 'Behold me standing at the door' and sang it very well only sometimes she did not open her mouth sufficiently wide and sang through her teeth. One of the young men singers I met in Corral and he knew me at once. He is a teacher at the school.

The other day at dinner on the shore, a little child 4 years of age was amusing half a dozen Captains with her sailor's talk. Another Captain and I were coming out and she shut the door on us and would not let us go. after amusing ourselves for a little while with her, we passed out and she called us back like this, 'I say Old Man, come back and sit down'. I said to the other man, 'She is calling you back'. He of course was just as certain it was me she meant; and we haven't yet settled who is right.

So you think to puzzle me with your G.F.S., but you don't; I have heard of it before, so your penny is lost. If I was being sarcastic, I would probably explain it as a General Foolish society, but as I certainy approve of Mrs G's efforts amongst the young girls, I hope the Girls Friendly Society may benefit them very much, both for this life and the life hereafter.

There is just a possibility, but not a probability, of me going up to Vancouver or Columbia River for salmon should things be better up there than here.

I have been wondering how you got on with your songs, if you broke down in them or not. Coudn't your Aunt help you to practice them? I don't know that I will be able to write to anyone else at Crosby this mail, so you must remember me to them and at Birkby Moor also. I got Aunt H's second letter, also got some papers from Charlie but no letter.

With kind love to all, I remain your Father,
T. Messenger.

Barque 'Midas', Valparaiso,   *August 30th 1896.*

My Dear Daughter,

This is another Sunday and a dull rainy one this evening. I always go to Bethel in the morning with the boys and after service, they spend some little time singing any hymn the boys like to name. Today, someone called for that Scottish one, 'It's a bonny, bonny world' and there was a little laugh when the Minister asked to be excused as the choir could not get their tongues round it.

This afternoon, I had my old shipmate of many years ago, who is now Captain MacDonald and his wife and son and another boy on board to tea. But it set in to rain and they would get wet going on shore. The boys were delighted to get a good run round the ship. You can tell M.J. that the papers for Willie have not come yet, so we did not see any one in Funny Times. How the editor of such a paper can get anyone to buy it, I don't know, as it is made up of such ridiculous trash.

My Mate is still in Hospital but will likely be on board ship tomorrow or I hope so. I am sure we will be here for two months more yet before I will be ready to leave. Mrs MacDonald today thought she would just like to have voyage to sea in a ship like this. She was delighted with the cabin.

I hope that Mr Marsh lets you get home in good time from his parties. If he doesn't, he will soon have your two Aunt Hanna's and Grandma after him. I fancy I remember something about him keeping his visitors until very late or very early

There are plenty of English people here in Valparaiso, but I think that the majority of them are pretty stuck up, putting on 'consequential airs' and not very sociable. The people here are very much afraid there will be a row over the election of a President. The two candidates were equal at first, but the second time one got a few more votes than the other. However the defeated ones say they are wrong votes and so the parties are bitter against each other. Today is the finishing day and everything is quiet enough in Valaparaiso, but there may be a row up at the capital, Santiago.

Hoping this finds you all at the Lodge quite well, I am your loving father,

     T. Messenger.

Barque 'Midas',   Valparaiso,   September 1896.

My Dear Daughter,
I have been in very bad fettle (as they say in Cumberland) this last few days, owing to a very bad cold in the head. Caught I think by sitting in the public square watching the fashions and the different shades of complexion amongst the natives here. The lowest class are a very dark yellow-brown colour and between them and the Europeans there is a vast variety of shades.

This month of September is a great holiday month. Today is one and they tell me next week there are four more and they will probably take the week, so we will not get on much with our discharging, probably not this month. But as times are, it will not matter much unless they want to send the ship up the coast to look for cargo, which they will probably eventually have to do.

For two nights I could hardly hold my head up, it was such a weight with the cold in it, but I hope to get a nights rest tonight and tomorrow it will be better.

When the last mail arrived here, there was only one solitary letter for the ship, for one of the boys, so I told Willie there was likely nothing fresh about Crosby.

I have just had a look on deck to see what the weather was like, but the wind seemed to blow clear through me, so I had to come down again. The engines on the line here astern of us are the greatest nuisance; they are tooting and whistling the whole night through.

Our boys are not the greatest oarsmen and now and again they catch a 'crab' and get knocked head over heels, to the great amusement of the boat men on the Landing Place. Or sometimes they strike some other boatmen's oar and are served the same. This evening, coming off, we had a strong wind against us and the boys, Willie among them, all got wet with the sprays blowing over them from the oars.

I am thankful my cold is so much better today, though my voice is not yet in singing order. I only found this pen-wiper you gave me in my coat pocket the other day. I often wondered what I had done with it.

10th.

I have just received some letters from Australia today, brought by a vessel just arrived from Newcastle, NSW and I am very pleased to hear from my friends there. Mrs Knight tells me her visit to the 'Ladas' at Newcastle afforded both pleasure amd profit to her, as she had many visitors from Newcastle at Katoomba during last Summer. She had gone away to Melbourne on a two month visit and was enjoying herself very much. By what she says, all the girls will soon be married. There is more work for the men in her family than for many years past and Katoomba must be in a flourishing condition as there are many new houses going up there.

As your birthday will soon be at hand, I must wish you all the happiness good for you in all the succeeding years that you may live. And that in after years, when looking backwards over your life, you may be able to say 'I am glad I have made someone happier than they would have been'; and that no past act in your life you may wish you had not done. We all do many acts in our lives, apparently trivial, that we still wish we had not done and blush when we think of them. I am afraid I ought to blush for a great many mean actions and do some times.

Sunday Sept. 13th.

I managed to get to Bethel this morning as it was very fine, but this afternoon it is blowing hard right into the Bay and raising up a big sea, so that some of the small vessels are throwing each end of themselves clean out of the water. It will take a day or two now to get the sea smooth enough for the launches to come for cargo.

Monday 14th September.

Still blowing from the North and a big sea up. Have not been able to get on shore to post letters today, so I don't know if these letters will go by the mail tomorrow or not. I expect some letters on Thursday by the mail in here as you would likely write after hearing of my arrival here.

With kind love to you and regards to your grandparents and Aunt H. I remain your loving Father,

T. Messenger.

Barque 'Midas'. Valparaiso,   October 23rd 1896.

My Dear Daughter,
I will soon be at sea out of this now and should be in San Francisco soon after you receive this. So you can write at once; you can get the address from Ritson's. We have had the ship dry-docked and painted and the bottom was covered all over with shells. She showed some dents in the iron plates where she had struck the rocks on the passage out. Just enough to show us what a narrow escape we had. However she is nice and clean now and should do some good sailing up the coast and along the SE Trades.

Now the fine Summer weather is coming on here and we are going up into Winter weather at San Francisco, though it does not get very cold there. I expect to sail tomorrow morning if I can find any money to pay my debts with here.

I did not get to the Bethel last Sunday, as we went into dock on that day and I was busy all morning.

Letters will not take so long to come to England from Frisco as from here.

You did not tell me if you were holding a Jubilee on your Grandpa's birthday; surely he had a party. If not, he may as well be at sea on his birthday.

Hoping you are quite well, with kind regards to your Grandparents and your Aunt H. I remain your Father,
                                        T. Messenger.

Barque 'Midas',   Sunday January 24th, 1897.

My Dear Daughter,
Just a fortnight tonight since we got down to Astoria from Portland and we got over the Bar out to sea next evening at 4 o'clock. The tug boat let us go just outside the whistling buoy and very soon it fell calm and we lay rolling about within sound of that screeching buoy until about 4 o'clock next morning, when the wind came at once quite strong with heavy rain. A fair wind from the NW and we let the Midas go for all she was worth on her way rejoicing.

Well that fair wind has never stopped and has brought us well on our way up here. Although it has only been very light this last week, so that I am only two days ahead of my passage to Victoria today, 13 days out. Still, no cause to grumble yet awhile, we improve it between here and the Equator. I am very glad to have had such fine weather; you see we have not so many men as we had and what we have are only boys or youths. So if we get bad weather, it means more work.

I hope you will get the pictures I sent all right in time for your bazaar.

Sunday 31st Jan. Lat. 4 N, Long. 118 W.
Only a poor run for this week but not bad for this part of the ocean. Our troubles have only started yesterday and today, that is calms and heavy showers, so that we are making little progress. I only hope it will not be for long and that we get hold of the SE Tradewinds soon.

We have another Barque to keep us company today, as there has not been wind enough for either to beat the other or bring us near enough to signal. We also had a good sized shark following us this afternoon. When the ship was moving a little, we tried to catch it with a piece of pork on a hook but His Sharkship was not hungry, or he objected to pork. At any rate, he did not come near enough to smell it, but disdainfully turned tail and left.

The weather is now very hot. Three weeks ago it was just too cold and probably in three weeks it will be cold again. I feel the ship keeling over a bit, which tells me there is a breeze, if it only lasts. The rain has stopped (the breeze did also very soon).

Monday.
Signalled the French Barque 'Reine Blanche' from San Francisco for Falmouth, 16 days out.

Sunday 7th February 1897.
Very fine weather, gentle breeze and clear sky and the ship going along so easy; scarcely a motion out of her. Today we made 120 miles; last voyage down here we were tearing along at 240 miles a day. Our breeze is strengthening a little tonight, so tomorrow we will have better work I hope.

It is still very hot and will be for 10 days or a fortnight, as we have to pass under the sun yet. But it can not get much hotter than it has been this past week. I believe that the men caught a bonita or two last evening at sun-down. They usually weigh about 14 pounds each and generally bite at dusk or when it is showerey. We have as companions today three white birds. The sailors call them Bosuns, on account of the long white tail feathers they carry. We have no vessels in sight and so have the ocean to ourselves as far as we can see. We only need clothing now to help keep the sun off us.

Sunday February 14th.
Made moderately fair progress this last week and I am in hopes of sighting Ducie Island tomorrow at noon. But I may easily miss it as it is so low, the tops of the trees only 26 feet above the water, so it can not be seen more than ten miles off from the mast head. Of course I am not anxious to see it; only as it lies in my way, I may as well look and see if any shipwrecked people are on it, though there is no water to be found on it. It is about 2 miles long and one mile broad and has a lagoon in the centre of it, leaving just a narrow fringe of dry land around it.

I am still three days less time out than I was in the Ladas when I passed Henderson Island, 150 miles to the West of this one, so I hope I may continue to keep ahead. We may soon get into cold weather again now; in fact the little rain showers we have had today felt quite chilly. The day we passed under the sun, we had quite a storm for a couple of hours; wind, rain, thunder and lightning. The rain was just a little deluge and the thunder overhead was terrifically jubilant; one peel answering another and then joining together in one wild uproar of sound. Every clap you could feel the ship tremble. The lightning, also in a state of delirium, flashing in all directions as usual before each peel of thunder. So Goodnight,

Monday 15th Feb.
At noon we should have been within 4 to 5 miles of the island but could not see it, so our Longitude is out some. I went up the mizen or after mast myself and had a good look but could see nothing; the coming down again nearly broke my legs. I thought I would drop on deck through the legs giving under me. It shows I must practice

going up and down the rigging to get the stiffness out of my joints. I am getting too lazy and too fat. A ship passed at dark bound North, likely from Australia for San Francisco.

Sunday February 21st.
We are now approaching a cold weather region, though we still have it warm. But this will likely be the last Sunday we will walk the decks bare-footed for some time. We have had very fine weather and light winds all this week and no birds about to keep us company. I noticed all the boys and some of the men rigged out with new caps, made of someone's old wool muffler apparently; just cut in lengths, sewn up and adorned with a many-coloured tassel. They spent their time on Sunday afternoon making them.

I was just 14 days from here to Cape Horn in the Ladas and I hope to do it again in the same time; I am still 4 days ahead of her time so far. We will soon have to look out our cold weather clothes, as it may turn cold all at once. The thermometer dropped a full 10 degrees in the last 24 hours, on account of the wind shifting. I have just been on deck and frightened the wind away, so I came below again.   Goodnight.

Sunday 28th February.
Very nasty rainy night but a fine fair wind blowing and the good Ship Midas is travelling along in a lively manner towards Cape Horn and I hope by next Sunday will be near it. We are going along steadily all the time, doing fair work every day. But the last three days were very uncomfortable for me, with the ship rolling so much when I got into bed, I had to reach out and hold onto the bed head for dear life or I would get tumbled out onto the deck. We are having a little colder weather now but still warm for the position we are in and we are not likely to have any real cold weather this passage; this month down here being like the month of August back home.

The other day, when the weather was clear and fine, we had quite a number of very large albatrosses about. They followed us for several days and although we never see them after dark, yet at daylight they are always around, or before sunrise at least. So their power of vision must be wonderful, the ship travelling perhaps 20 miles in the night. I have to put on my spectacles now to see to write between the lines here and in fact I am beginning to have to use them a good deal. It is very pleasant to sit here and listen to the swish of the water along the side as the ship is rushing through it at the rate of over 10 knots an hour; and going along so easy I will not need to hold onto the bedstead tonight. As for the rain, that does not trouble me, as I am not going out in it.

Sunday Night March 7th.
At last we are round Cape Horn. We have got a fine northerly wind which is not altogether favourable, but will do us for a day or so. I am just five days ahead of the Ladas time, so I hope I may keep the advantage all the way home. The other day we had a very heavy gale and the Midas was filled up with water fore and aft and I think mostly everyone had a good washing round in it, the ropes getting all over the side through the ports. Fortunately it was not very cold. I was steering myself for a while and I have hardly got over the unusual exertion, at least my right hand has not. A German Barque passed to the Westward this forenoon, from Liverpool for Hono-lulu. This breeze we have is favourable for her. We are hoping to run up into warm weather soon, but the wind must change first for us. There are not many birds about now but the same albatross is still with us. Today, although the ship was going through the water at 11 miles an hour at the time, the porpoises were just playing round and round as if in derision at our slow speed. They jumped clean out of the water and wriggled their tails in a most comical fashion; hilariously joyful. We have no harpoon on board or we could easily have got one. 11 o'clock has gone, so Goodnight to you.

Monday 8th March.
Took soundings and found 70 fathoms depth with a bottom of grey sand. Some porpoises swimming around idly in a lazy kind of manner because it is calm.

Sunday 14th March 1897.
Well we have been trying to make up for two days calm, but I am still a day behind the Ladas from Cape Horn. We have had a very good breeze for the last four days and made good work throughout

and I am in hopes of soon overtaking my last time up here.

The weather is now quite warm again and the porpoises have changed colour. Cape hens and albatross are quite numerous about today. The ship is leaning over so much now I can not sleep in bed, so I take the sofa and do better on that. In fact my time is mostly occupied in sleeping and trying to sleep, chiefly the latter.

Have not seen a single ship since last Sunday but it has been foggy a great deal, so we could not see far several times. I was very much afraid of ice, but if we passed any we did not see it. I should be at the Equator in another three weeks; I hope so.

Sunday 21st March.

A very pleasant day but ending up not quite so pleasant, as it has come up squally and threatening unknown things. So at 8 o'clock I have made snug all the upper sails to await events, as the sea is rising more than the wind at present.

We are near the position of the Ladas when she nearly capsized on us last voyage. But the Midas is not so ticklish as she was. We have had a nice day since noon and I am regretting this disagreeable change as it stops my anticipated day's run. Proving the old proverb not to reckon the chickens before they are hatched; a thing I am very prone to.

We have made good progress this last week for the place we have sailed across. I have gained one day from Cape Horn on the Ladas and hope I may gain more by the time I cross the Equator if this sudden change does not last too long.

We are now into very warm weather again, no covering needed at nights sleeping. If it was not for the brisk breeze we have had it would be very hot indeed.

Two of our new hands in the coal hole got to work fighting down there and came up with their eyes blacked otherwise than with coal dust. One of them was a chemist's assistant but at present he looks more like a Liverpool corner boy. This sea is getting up so bad it is making me sea sick.

Sunday 28th March.

All the distance made this week we have had to work for in a zig-zag fashion; East and West aginst light Northerly winds and frequent heavy rains. Still we are not apparently any nearer the Trades, though well inside of where they should be. Today a small group of vessels have been crossing and re-crossing within signalling distance of us and two we recognised from Portland a week before us. Another was from New Zealand for London, the Waitangi, a Maori name. This evening at dusk made out the signals of a Whitehaven ship most likely from Brisbane, Queensland.

We are struggling to get North and looking long for trade Winds. We have been so bothered with the wind shifting about, causing us to turn the ship around tacking, that I did not get a wash, only with the showers. My legs ache with walking about the deck so much. My head aches with heat and closeness; and my hand hurts from a small boil on it. So altogether I have had a weary day, with the worrying about wind added to all else. Nonetheless I rejoice that we are all well on board and daily make some progress nearer home; just 500 miles this week.

Sunday April 4th.
A beautiful day, fine brisk Trade winds blowing the Midas along at nearly 200 miles a day. I hope in two days more to cross the Equator into the North Atlantic Ocean; then I shall feel we are getting nearer home every day. We have not seen a vessel since we got the Trades and left them all behind us. I trust we will keep ahead of them for the remainder of the way home and I hope that this day in five weeks we will be very near our Port of Falmouth or Queenstown.

The sun is very hot and were it not for the breeze blowing, we would be nearly roasted. As it is, the thermometer registers 83 degrees F. in the cabin now, with a fine breeze blowing through at 10 o'clock at night. Consequently it is well on in the morning before I can get to sleep.

I hear that the boys have already made up their minds as to how many and what kinds of new suits they will have when they get home. Willie has been chief helmsman this passage in the day time.

Sunday April 11th.
Plenty of rain last night and today and some thunder and lightning. Doldrum weather and a change after the great heat we have been

having. Making very little progress this last five days and now I am anxiously looking for the NE Trades. There are a number of other ships about in the same predicament. Yesterday we tried to catch a young shark, but it would not bite the pork. Today we tried to catch a big fellow, but he did not get on the hook properly and so got away. Although he came round the hook for a full hour afterwards, he was too cautious to bite again. Probably his jaw was sore.

A ship we passed on the Equator five days ago is still in sight of us yet. Although we leave her behind every day, we get becalmed and she comes up to us again with the faint breezes. When we do get a breeze, the Midas can pass her very fast; she is called the Nelson of Glasgow from Canterbury, New Zealand bound for London. She has proved a bad companion for us, as we have had no wind since we passed her. I don't suppose we have made 10 miles in a right direction in the last 24 hours. Calms and heavy rains all day today. Plenty of rain water for the boys to wash their clothes and a queer sample of washing they do.

Sunday 18th April.
Another week over and we have made a better distance in a right direction, having had the Tradewind all week but not very strong. From the position we are in today, last voyage I was 25 days to Liverpool. We are just the same time out, but I hope we will be a few days less this time to Falmouth. We may easily do so, as I spent 7 days doing nothing around this vicinity last time. Only a few flying fish about. Any ship we come across does not keep company long with us. They are soon left behind out of sight and yet I grumble at the Midas for being so slow. While no doubt the people in the ships we pass will think we are very fast. The men are busy painting the ship all round and from the mast head down so that she will be acceptable for going into Port.

Sunday 25th April.
Another week and still the Trades stick to us long after I expected to be rid of them. The consequence is we have lengthened our distance considerably for although we have been going on all the week, we are not much nearer the Channel then last Sunday. We are in a position now for fair winds from the West and although it

is calm at present mainly, yet I hope that a breeze will not be long in coming.

120 days out but we have near two thousand miles to go yet. We are nearly through the Sargasso Sea and leaving the Gulf Weed behind us; a weed that floats on the ocean 2/3rds across the Atlantic and over a breadth varying from 700 to 1500 hundred miles. A few lazy porpoises around at sundown tonight and all heading NE ward.

All our potatoes are finished today so will have to turn to beans and rice alone now. Someone caught a sparrow hawk, a young one the other day, but it is probably dead now as it refused to eat anything.

Sunday May 2nd.
We are still a very long way from Port yet, our progress this last week being but slow. Today was the best run for a long time; 150 miles in a right direction. We have been just playing with a lot of other vessels, passing them and rapidly leaving them out of sight when we got a breeze. When we had only a light air, they would all come up along side again. So today with a breeze we have been leaving them all and repassing one that had got ahead again

The French 4-mast ship Union bound for Hamburg, 77 days out and a very fine ship she is, but the Midas is too fast for her in a breeze. Another very large 4-master keeps up very well with us. I take her to be the Windermere (Fisher and Sprotts), but I may be mistaken. He was just too far off to read the flags. We had six ships in front and six behind us today.

There is not much chance of us making Port by next Sunday now without a very good fair wind all the way, which we are not likely to get. However we will do our very best and get there as soon as ever we can. The sea is so smooth that the ship is gliding along near 8 knots, with scarce a move out of her to indicate that she was going through the water at all. I noticed the sailors throwing their old clothes over the side yesterday, a sign that they think the voyage is nearly up and all the painting and tarring done. So it is, but the difficulty is to keep it clean now.

I hope to be able to finish this for you in Falmouth in 10 days at least, as I know you will be beginning to count the days to my arrival. So Goodnight.

Sunday 9th May 1897.

I am properly sick and disgusted with the little progress we have made this week and now we have a fresh breeze dead ahead from the East. Our only consolation is that we had no less than 17 other vessels in sight today, all as bad as ourselves.

The other day the ship I thought to be the Windermere was closer to and we found it was the Manchester. So I put our boat out and went on board to dinner with the Captain (Hicks). His wife and son are on board and a boy 4 years old. They were very nice, so I stopped on board until 2 o'clock and got some books from them as well. I had a view of the Midas under sail and thought she looked very well indeed. Mrs Hicks was very anxious to get home, though they are 6 days less time out than we are. They told me the Auchencairn sailed two days before them so she will be around here somewhere. Also the ship is pitching into a head sea very disagreeably.

Sunday 16th May.

The ship is pitching again the same as she was last Sunday and very nearly to as little purpose, as the wind is still ahead of us. We had it fair one day last week and altogether we have got nearly 400 miles nearer to Falmouth, with 500 to go.

We have had no vessels with us since last Sunday except one Norwegian we passed today. We have been watching every change of the moon for the last month and hoping for a fair wind. Every change, we get a breeze, but it is always ahead. Then we may chance to get a light air favourable to help us on a 100 miles or so. Then it will die out and the whole thing is repeated. Probably just when we have struggled on to within a short distance of Port, the Westerly winds will be coming after us. Today it is full moon and we have got a fine Easterly breeze and we may make the most of it. As day after day passes by, I hardly know what to do with myself; even washing myself I am afraid it is more for something to pass the time than from habits of cleanliness.

We had two swallows on board the other day and night, so I shut one in my book case at dark. It stopped quiet enough all night, but at daylight it got fluttering at the glass trying to get out, so I got up and let it out in the saloon.

Sunday 23rd May 1897.
Still 200 miles off either Falmouth or Queenstown and still the wind is right East against us. This last week, we never had one hours favourable slant, but have had to beat to windward for every mile made good. At the same rate it will be next Saturday before we arrive and yet a very small change of wind would carry us into Queenstown.

Some steamboats passed us the other day, so we should be reported in tomorrow's paper, if not today's. Then Mr Ritson will see that we are near at hand. I was looking over our small stores the other day and found left,

     6 bottles of pepper
     2 bottles of table salt
     6 bottles of pickles
     also some baking powder.

The only thing we have left to eat to our meat and bread is oatmeal and rice, enough for three days more in the cabin. For the others, all they have is flour and salt meat, butter and marmalade. So its time we were into Port and had some more oatmeal.

I know you will be looking anxiously for my arrival every day. We always have a good breeze on Sundays, right ahead though. The day we were 120 days out, I made the angry remark that now we were so long, I didn't care a fig if we were 140 days out. At present it appears as if we would be fully that time out before we can reach Port. It takes a long while to beat up 200 miles, especially when it so often falls nearly calm.

The swallows we had about have died from cold I suppose, as it is very cold at night time. A few old ragged-winged gulls and big gannets are about in daytime, but we do not see any of the ships around that were with us for so long. Possibly we cross each other in the dark.

I did think we should have been home for the Queen's birthday, but we won't. I fancy all the boys are homesick, this being so near and can't get in; it is trying to them, as well as annoying to me. Still, everyone is well and our passage is not yet terribly long. So we need not grumble much; it is being so near that is the trouble.

138

Limerick River,   Sunday 30th May 1897.

My Dear Daughter,

We are just now on our way up the Shannon towards Limerick, having made a much better passage round from Falmouth than I expected with the wind as it was when we left there. I am in some doubt if we will be able to get right up to turn or not as the tides are low, but we will only stick in the mud and not do any hurt to the ship. So I am taking the risk of it if we have to lighten ship to get up.

I wrote you from Falmouth but forgot to address the letter, so unless the pilot had sense to send it to Mr Ritson for you, you will not have got it. I am sorry the photographer did not send you those photos, but I have some with me. I am glad to see you succeeded in passing, if it was only in third degree; next time you may do better. All the lads will be a little disappointed because they will have to make another passage before they get home, but they will be pleased we are coming to Maryport.

When do your holidays commence? I will not be able to leave here by the Jubilee time I am afraid.

There, the ship has just stuck in the mud and the tug boat can not move us. She was going ahead over it so nicely, that I thought we were all right. Now we are likely to have to take out cargo to get off.

We have got off all right, but have to go back to anchor in deep water.

Willie has just told me they have put off the Sunday School trip for him to be home, but he will not be there unless they put it off longer yet. I wonder, can you get away from school to come over here or not? I am not sure that Mr Ritson would care about you going round in the ship, so I do not exactly know if it is worthwhile having you over supposing you could get away.

With kind regards to your Grandparents and Aunt H.

I remain your loving Father,   *T. Messenger.*

I will go up to Limerick with the tug tonight to see how things look on Sundays here. Kind regards to next door and Birkby Moor.

Barque Midas, Limerick   *Saturday.*

My Dear Daughter,
I had your letter a day or two late as, at the office, they had been put
on one side and forgotten on the day we docked. It took me some
time to read all those Australian letters, as they had to tell me all
about the weddings that will have taken place by this time. So my
friends are increasing in number there fast.

I see you have heard of Limerick lace. I wasn't going to say
anything about it for fear you should want some, but some one else
has told you. Well my Little Princess, how many hundred yards of
very best Irish Point lace can I send you. I may be in a school this
afternoon when they make it and I can order an unlimited quantity.
You forgot to tell me Cousin M. McCarty had got married and Aunt
H. just says you will have told me all about it. No matter, happy girl.
I dare not make fun any more, or give impudence to her. I can only
wish her much happiness.

Monday is a holiday here, Whit Monday and I shall probably go
out for a run somewhere. How I wish I could run a bicycle. Captain
Nelson says he has just had to order one for his eldest girl, about
your age. I said what a mercy my girl could not ride one

Of course it is quite possible we may be in Maryport in time for
the Jubilee celebrations. Willie can then enjoy himself to his fullest
extent with all his chums.

Trusting yourself, Aunt H., Grandmother and Father and all the
family, are well. I remain your loving father,
                    T. Messenger.

Barque Midas, Limerick,   *Wednesday.*

My Dear Daughter,
Your letter reached me at noon today. I am pleased to note your
Aunt H. is not so very stout and heavy that she would be in danger
of breaking a bicycle down. I never suggested or hinted at the
possibilty of such an alarming catastrophe occurring. I am told that
Aunt H. was on one at Crosscannonby, a good machinist, out to
pedal well on a bicycle. You seem to have lots of friends, ready to

help you to learn and I expect you to be a good rider soon if you practice. Possibly I will have a visit from the Crosby church Army Bicycle Brigade, headed by the Rev. Mr Marsh himself. in the event of such an occurrence, I have laid in a stock of good hard San Francisco biscuits from the Auchencairn here. I am much afraid that, if you learn to run a bicycle, you will not win a prize next exam you have.

It has been very wild and showery the last two days here and has delayed us very much with getting in ballast, so that I do not expect to get away from here for a week yet. I was hoping to leave on Saturday, but there is no chance of that now, as I haven't got 70 tons of stone in the ship yet. So you will have plenty of time to write me again before I sail. I am sorry to miss all the grand festivities you are going to have, but you must just enjoy yourself as well as you can without me.

I don't know what there is to do here if anything, at all, at all. My cold is now a vast deal better, but still not clear yet. Coming round the dock on Sunday evening, we were just passing the Barque Magnet and two ladies were in front of us. One read the name of the vessel and said 'Magnet, yes Magnet is a very good bicycle'. I thought the Captain would have been much offended to have his vessel likened to a bike, if he had heard it.

It is so cold today that I will have to light the cabin fire if it continues. I haven't got the Irish lace for you; I am afraid I can not afford it this time. Trusting you are quite well, I remain your loving father,   *T. Messenger.*

Barque Midas, Limerick Dock.   *Wednesday.*

My Dear Daughter,
I got your letter this morning and am quite amused at your wants.

I dare not buy you a bicycle, because your Aunt H. Menhams might learn to ride it first and run off with it. The piano can wait awhile; the umbrella I can promise you, also your own choice.

We have finished cargo tonight and I will go into dry dock Friday morning. Then I have 500 tons of ballast to take in and that will take us all next week to get on board. Then I hope we will have quick passage round.

I think Mary Lizzie must have waited until I left places before she wrote to me. I don't expect to have much time to go far visiting when we get to Maryport, as we will be loading up rapidly.

I think I told you that the Mate's wife was here on board and I would like to know, what does it matter to Willie where H. Pattinson goes to? Do you think he will fret about it; not him.

I have not got any lace for you yet, but will try for some one of these days. I have got all my hair cut off and my whiskers chopped short, so look most highly respectable, like a doctor or lawyer, rather than a sailor.

Kind regards to all at Crosby; your new Schoolmistress also when she comes. And love to yourself, from your loving father,   T. Messenger.

Did you ever get my letter from Falmouth or not?

Barque Midas, Limerick.   *Wednesday, 23.6.97.*

My Dear Daughter,

You have likely been too busy keeping up the Jubilee celebrations to write again. Well we had some litle amusement here too yesterday. The vessels in the dock were all gaily decorated with flags and the principal places about the town. But I believe in the rough Irish part of the town they put out a black flag or two and there was a bit of a row when the police went to take them down. Some wag had moored a plank in the middle of the river, with a black flag upon it and a gallant member of the Royal Irish Constabulary Force bravely swam out and took down the obnoxious thing. I decorated myself with the jubilee bow, red white and blue; and felt myself unique as I walked up the street, with not another one to be seen and all the people looking at me.

Last evening there was a Military Tattoo and torchlight procession in the barrack grounds. There are a lot of soldiers here, the best part of the Royal Irish Regiment. So they gave a little entertainment for charitable purposes and it was very nice. After we left, we called at a gentleman's house for a short while. Then we all came down to the docks and gave them some fireworks, burned blue lights and fired off a few rockets for our friends amusement. Then we saw them out of the dock gate and on their way home at 1 a.m. this morning.

We are not going to get away out of this before Saturday, they are so wretchedly slow at putting in our ballast. I am trying to remember when I had a letter from Crosby and also when I wrote one. We had Mr Ritson here from Friday until Monday night and I am glad he was here to see for himself what it was detained me from getting away.

I really think the boys are not at all anxious to leave Limerick, as I see they all have got sweethearts here, the boys from the Auchencairn also. Indeed I have been thinking of looking up one for myself.

I got you quite a stock of lace yesterday; I won't say what kind but no doubt Aunt H. will think me foolish and say it is too good for you, a young girl, to wear.

With kind love, hoping soon to be with you, I remain your loving Father.   *T. Messenger.*

U.K. TO NAGASAKI, 1897.

Barque Midas, off Holyhead.   *Wednesday (Aug. 97).*

Dear Mary Adelaide,

At last I am fairly away to sea again and on the whole just a little pleased to be so. We anchored off Maryport last night to get our damage repaired and did not get started until 11 o'clock We passed St Bee's Head 2 o'clock in the morning, so the Ramsays would not see me going past.

I am addressing this to Crosby, as you will likely be there by the time this reaches you. I hope you were not scared too much when the Midas made such a rush at the lighthouse and put a hole in it. It will be a long time before you will have any word from me again, but I have no doubt we will reach Nagasaki all in due time. So do not be in the least alarmed for us.

We have a nice little favourable breeze and as soon as I reach Holyhead, I will cast off the tug and go alone; as you did on the bicycle. I think the Misses Broadbent would be tired by the time they got home again after racing so fast to see the ship out.

You will not need to post any letters for at least three months and a half for the Midas, so you will have plenty of time to write a good long one. When you write to Mrs Holmes, remember me most kindly to her and Emily also.

I can not say much more to you, except mind your lessons and pass your exams in a creditable manner and do credit to your teachers. I know you will not ride on the bicycle too much. Tell your Aunt H. that the offer to her stands for twelve months, so she has plenty of time to learn.

I find I have actually come away without any ink, so I will have to write less this passage. I think we have a very good crew; at least they shape well so far, if they only continue it. Our breeze is getting better and better and I hope it will take us out of Channel at the very least.

It is now nearly dinner time, so we will not be much longer getting to the Head and casting off the tug. So I must conclude with

Nagasaki   Jan 1st/1898

My dear daughter

                    This is New Years
night, & today, I have not been on shore
at all. it has been raining more or less
all day & is continuing it on tonight
as in last-night before the New Years
most of my men have been on shore &
are ashore yet I suppose & Willie also
has had his first run on shore today
he got out-fine after dinner but did not
hold up for long. so the boys would not
have a nice walk. Although I have
been here nearly a fortnight your
letters have not yet come to hand
so unless your uncle John has been mistaken
about-you having written I cannot make
out-where the letters have got-to.
There has not-been any great display
of Bellringing or firing of primrose
here to commemorate the New Year
and it-has been so wet-that I have
not-troubled to fire a rocket. myself
The rain has at-last-brought much

145

best love, from your Father, *T. Messenger*.

When we reached the Island of Anglesey it fell calm and a thunder storm got up on the land and we had some heavy rain. Since then it has been much cooler. At Holyhead it was quite calm, so I let the tugboat go on with us for Bardsey Island and I will cast off there. That is 35 miles from Holyhead if you look at it on the map. Of course if it is calm down there, I may proceed on to Tuskar. It is very fine now and a gentle breeze blowing, but it may not last long.

With love again, I am your Father.
Tugboat leaving off Bardsey at 9.30 pm.

Barque 'Midas', at sea off Cape Verde Islands, Aug.22nd 1897.

My Dear Daughter,
It will soon be 2 weeks since we sailed and I see that I am near the same position I was on the last voyage at the same time out. Well so far we have come along in a very easy style and I hope we shall not be delayed any but go right on to the Equator.

At present our Trade winds are only light because we are near the Islands but they may freshen up again soon as we are past them. So far we are all quite well and the boys were trying their vocal powers, singing hymns this evening, so I suppose they were happy. But what a long, long way we have to go yet, over 16,000 miles the route I will have to take. I try not to think of it, that I may not get disheartened about it; and I say to myself, no matter, we will reach out there in time.

Mrs Holmes sent me a box of books and other things. I have only had time so far to look at them, as I am reading all your Pearson's first, then the Sunday Companions and other equally interesting papers your Aunt H. has put up, such as Women's Lives. I wonder how you are getting on with your bicycle and if you are tired of it yet or not.

Sunday 29th August.
The rain is pattering on the deck over my head and it has been raining more or less all day. We also had a brisk and favourable

breeze with it; now it is nearly calm. We are just now crossing the belt of several degrees of doldrums; that is variable breezes and calms, but at this season mainly from the SW and called South-west Monsoons. I am still 300 miles from the Equator and am not going to cross it as soon as I did last voyage; still I can not complain. I am hoping soon to be able to pick up the Trade wind, then away South we will go through them. Then we will be on the lookout for the winds to waft us along past the Cape of Good Hope and on round Australia; then up North through the SE Trades across the Line and into NE ditto, right up North to Japan. But Oh Dear, what a long way it is; even a good days run seems such a little bit out of the whole distance.

Sunday 5th September 98.
Now we are across the Equator this evening. I didn't see the line as we came across it, it is invisible. We have been getting along very slow this past week, but as we are now fairly in the SE Trades, we may hope to get along a bit faster for a week at least. I am finding this penwiper you made me very handy at nights now for smashing cockroaches with; they are getting so numerous about my lamp. Now, with this warm weather, the rats also are getting plentiful and leaving their tracks around the cabin and storeroom. I think I have got through all your weeklies and will try Sunday Companions next, for I am weary of doing nothing. I had better give up command and go Mate again.

Sunday 12th September 98.
A good week's run this week. Passed Trinidad Island today 60 miles off and did not get any butterflies, the wind being in the wrong direction and the weather too cold. It is quite chilly again in the evenings and mornings; our Trades seem broken up today and the weather looks like a change. I only hope the wind will not come unfavourable for us. Although we saw no land today we had a number of strange birds about us, birds that never go far off the land. We have not seen many ships about lately; seem to have the road pretty much to ourselves.

Sunday Sept. 19th. 98.
Another Sunday passed away nearly and the Midas keeps on her way, making more or less distance daily, mostly very little this week. At present we have a light pleasant fair wind and smooth sea. I am grumbling because the wind is too fair, for with light winds behind her the Midas is a regular old barge for slowness. For instance, 3 days ago I passed a Barque (wind then on the side and light) very fast and left her nearly out of sight. Next day, the wind came aft behind us and up came the same Barque gradually. Today she is away ahead of us, a German vessel from Sweden for Melbourne and 66 days out. We are 47. The sun is still very hot in daytime and makes the deck too hot to walk barefooted, but the nights are very cool, so I get up in the morning and go on deck in the sun to warm my old bones up before venturing to have a good bath and rub down.

I am often wondering whether you have had a fall or broken your bicycle yet. Mrs Holmes will likely have got Emily one. It will soon be Winter and you will not be able to ride so much then.

The nearest land we have to pass will be the Island of Tristan da Cunha. I shall hardly see it. There are about 100 inhabitants and I believe they live a very good life. Not enough society for much wickedness. I would like to call there and see them but dare not risk any delay in my passage. We are about 700 miles off there yet.

So Goodnight.

Thursday 23rd Sept.
Passed the Islands today and could see the largest (8400 ft. high), 60 miles off. The day has been so fine and clear, I am sorry I did not go nearer and see the people.

Sunday 26th Sept. 97, 10pm.
Going 10 knots, fine fresh wind and clear weather, but today the ship has been doing some quick rolling. Just as you fancy she is nicely settled on one side for a minute or two, away she goes with a swing far over the other way. It makes me think of my efforts to learn to ride the bike. Only when the Midas takes a roll to one side, she always recovers herself again; the bike did not. I always had to

call for assistance to get it upright and then the united efforts of myself and a number of smaller and younger Messengers was insufficient to keep it so with myself in the saddle. No matter, I hope to do better next time.

I hope by next Sunday I will be past the Meridian of the Cape of Good Hope, as I am past the Meridian of Greenwich now or nearly on the Prime Meridian and our Longitude is zero. Now from here to Australia I have a run of over 6000 miles to do and I hope not to meet with any ice on the road. I had to make use of your penwiper to demolish an inquisitive cockroach. I don't see many now, it is so cold, but the heat from the lamp likely brought that one out to its demolishment.

When reading through this, don't think I have forgotten your birthday because I have said nothing about it; I was not able to send you a card.   Well Goodnight.

Sunday October 3rd, 1897.
I have just been on deck looking at the weather and seeing how the ship is going and I find things favourable all round. The ship is going right before a fine pleasant gale, not rolling too much, only a very easy gentle roll. The weather is a little hazy and rainy with the moon showing through it; it is also nice and warm and all serene. We are well past the Cape now and hope to go along in good style to past Australia (there, I had to stop writing to destroy a cockroach; the warmth from the lamp brings them out to their doom).

The ship was tumbling about a good lot the other day and I was struggling to keep my feet while washing in the bath. Then all at once she gave a kind of tarara-boom-de-ay twist and I went head first into my own stomach (the portraits) and nearly knocked the wind out of myself. I still keep myself up there and admire myself all by myself in the bathroom.

The weather has changed from very cold to warm this last two days. It will soon be cold with you in England also.   Goodnight.

Sunday October 10th, 97.
This has been an alarming, exciting and damaging day for us. Two of our best sails blown away to ribbons, only some fragments left.

It came on to blow a small hurricane last night at 9 o'clock. This morning it was blowing very hard until daylight. The main deck filled up with water all the time and I daresay the boys were nearly washed out of their place, as some of them went to sleep in the forecastle. They have been at work all day today clearing up and setting sails again, as the wind has moderated gradually and at present we are going along very nicely again at 8-9 knots. We have made this week 210 miles daily and hope we may keep it up for some time.

Two days ago was a very nasty forenoon, blowing fresh and raining. We were looking out anxiously for rocks, knowing we would pass very close to the Crozet Islands as I had been intending to see them and so we did. The Twelve Apostles loomed up through the fog all at once, probably just about a mile off. So we were just clearing them nicely and, as usual when I cared little whether it cleared up or not, it cleared up. A fine afternoon and we could have taken a good view of the Islands had it only cleared 4 hours before.

There are some more Islands further South we will pass, but I am going to keep clear of them. Most of the cockroaches are dead but I had my breakfast spoiled yesterday morning through one. I had just got nicely set to work on my rice when I got sight of one of them amongst it. It spoiled my temper as well as the breakfast.

Hoping we will not meet any more violent storms or any more disasters. I am your dutiful father, *T. M.*

Sunday October 17th.

A very light air blowing just at present and the Captain in a disagreeable temper in consequence. The ship is doing rolling enough for half a gale of wind. Just as I started writing now, down dropped a cockroach on to the paper. Probably it is many yards astern by this time. That reminds me that the Mate was telling me that whenever he takes his cap or boots off, they always go for the warm place and he finds them dropping on his head (he is like me on top so soon feels them) or crawling up his leg; they haven't done that with me yet.

Foolish boy Burnett, whose Mother did not know what ship he belonged to, brought his bed out to dry this afternoon. Lazy and careless-like, he dropped it in the handiest place just because it happened to be dry there at the time. Very soon, the ship found out there was something to be washed about; she filled up the decks and washed it round a bit for him. So it will be some time before he gets it dry again.

We have had very changeable unsettled weather this week; either too much or too little wind and too much sea. A Barque has been in company yesterday and today. I thought it was the Parkdale, but on getting nearer yesterday, I saw I was mistaken as she was much smaller though painted the same. She ran ahead of us last night; today we have passed her, as we carried more canvas. I could not make out any name and was too busy to signal and today she was too far away.

I was asking Willie if he had eaten all his cakes. He said Yes they were all done now; I have no doubt they have been done for some time. So I gave him a little piece of my gingerbread loaf from the Biscuit-Makers, Liverpool and just saved one little piece more for next Sunday. We still have 2200 miles to go to Tasmania, before we can turn up North into warm weather.

Sunday October 24th 97.

This has been a rather turbulent week for us and we have had a regular chapter of accidents, all through the fault of one little link giving way. I lost a good part of a brand new sail and got the Top Mast cut into severely with the yards swinging about on it. It was blowing hard on Monday night, but had settled at midnight. I turned in at 1 o'clock Tuesday morning, with the thought that the gale was settled and the ship going along in good shape, with nothing to trouble me. I had just about got settled after my third or fourth turnover, when I heard something carry away and a row of a fluttering sail. I didn't want any calling; I was on deck pretty sharp but there was a pretty mess up aloft. All the yards swinging about at once and we had a job to secure them, as the sea was breaking over the ship in all directions, washing people about.

So it has just taken us all the week to partly repair damages and get sails on the ship again. Today has been the finest we have had for a long time and the ship has had the least water on her decks. I hope the Midas has finished up with her breaking and destroying things now. I could have been 2-300 miles further along but for that defective link, one of the last I really expected to go.

Nevertheless we are going on our way all the time and may sight Australia in another five days or so if we continue to be favoured with such fine breezes. I think everyone will have got all their clothes dried today. I saw Willie had his donkey's breakfast out in the sun; and that reminds me I will just give him this last piece of cake now before I go to bed, as he is on deck at present, 11 pm.

October 31st 1997.

A fine pleasant Sunday again, after a few days of stormy, unpleasant weather and more damages done to the sails than we will be able to repair in a week's time. In rounding the South end of Tasmania, we had a hard gale and violent squalls off the land. Next day it was very fine and smooth water until near midnight. Then as we began to enter Basse's straits, another storm came on very rapidly and a terrible beam sea made things very uncomfortable and tried the masts and rigging very much. Some of our sails got blown away; that means sail making for all hands. Now we are getting North again into warmer weather, I hope to be able to go to work at them.

One old man, a Frenchman, had his leg hurt yesterday, by getting knocked about by a sea coming on board. The old chap has been laid up nearly all the way down here with his shoulder, due to a similar fall. As he is a good old sailor, I shall soon have him on deck again in fine weather. I have to let them know sometimes that I am not exactly running a convalescent Hospital in the Midas, but can find them work to suit their condition; that is the Lay-up Sailors, 'the halt, the lame and the blind'. The boys all stick to it bravely and seem to escape the seas wonderfully. Mr Richmond, the Mate, seems to catch the most wettings; the seas and sprays make a break for him the moment he comes on deck

How I wished I had been bound for Sydney when I saw the Light S. of Tasmania on Friday night, but have still 4,500 miles to go yet.

Sunday November 7th.

Still the good Barque Midas going on her way cheerily towards the Equator. We have been favoured much this week for the place we are in, not to have been stopped for a single day on our way up North. Now we have got hold of a fine Trade wind and will soon be abreast of New Caledonia. The Island belongs to France and they send convicts there. I don't intend to sight it and hope the land does not break the Trade wind up and leave us becalmed for any length of time, so spoiling a good passage I have made so far. It is excellent work to be in the position we are in 95 days.

I find my old sailor's leg is damaged more than I expected and he can not put his foot down on the deck yet. The weather is nice and warm now and the ship going along a good 8-9 knots, for which I am thankful.

I suppose the roads will not be good for bicycle riding now, so you will have so much more time for your lessons and your music, to get well forward with them. I don't see any cockroaches about my lamp now. I fancy I must have got them all killed in the cold weather, but we will likely soon get a new breed along from the Galley.

Sunday Nov. 14th 97.
A scorching hot day and very little wind. As we are now within the belt of Equatorial calms, we expect variable winds, calms and showers. Up to the present however, the breeze has kept favourable. In fact we have still got the Trades, only very faint; just made 74 miles in the last 24 hours.

On Friday morning at daylight, we were close alongside the Stewart Islands with a very nice breeze. I was watching to see if any canoes were coming off. I had just concluded we were going too fast, when young Light at the wheel saw two or three canoes ahead. Very soon they were hanging on alongside and the natives on board in a jiffy, though the ship was going six knots through the water at the time. They had a few shells and coconuts to trade with and wanted tobacco chiefly. The first two who came on board came up to me very mysteriously. Producing a letter, they invited me to come down the hold, meaning the cabin. So when I got there in the saloon, they shut the door to keep the others out. The letter was just a note from the Captain of another ship, to say he had been trading with the natives and they were very peaceable. It was dated the 4th, just eight days before us. I gave the fellows some tobacco, beef and and biscuits and got a few shells and coconuts in return. Willie had a canoe from them. As they wore no clothes, yet all had pipes, the only place they had to carry them when not smoking was through a hole in their ears, large enough for the purpose. I believe that the sailors and boys too, bartered all their table knives and forks away. They likely wanted them to cut the meat I gave them. The blacks had by far the best of the bargain, as I gave them a good supply of tobacco and bread and made swells of two of them at least by giving them a couple of handkerchiefs. They wanted some scent to put on them to be swells when they went on shore. I am inclined to think that the two fellows I gave tobacco to were keeping it all to themselves. The Guile-less Natives were not inclined to share with others on the boat. They would have about ten miles or more to go back to the Island, but their canoes go very fast and it was only 8 o'clock when they left us. They all spoke a few words of English and knew the names of things, but I would have been glad if they had only brought potatoes instead of coconuts. As they went away, the boys sung out, Goodbye, See you in Liverpool. It appears there was nobody in the ship had any pipes to give them, either of clay or wood.

The breeze is very faint, but I must not grumble as we are going the right way, if only slowly. I hope to cross the Equator in four days more; then I hope to be not longer than 30 days from thence to Port. If so, I will consider I have made a rattling good passage in under 140 days.

Monday Evening, 22nd November.
Still we are not at the Line yet. We have had no calms, only very light head wind and working our way to the Northward against it. At noon today, we were still 69 miles off; but the breezes being favourable, we may reach across it tomorrow. All last week we had a companion to race with, or drift with would be more correct, the wind being so light. Yesterday at daylight, she was gone out of sight, on the tack, I suppose.

The sun is like a furnace, glaring down upon us all day, but tonight the rain had cooled the ship. Still it is very hot in the cabin; I generally have a good deal of shifting about to find a cooler place each time. Firstly I try the chart house and it is HOT. Then I shift below and try the sofa and probably if the sun is on that side it is hotter still. Then I will try the bed and it will be the hottest of all, but I will be about desperate then. So I lay and perspire freely and grumble more freely, until just before daylight it gets a bit cooler and I get a little sleep.

Now the rain is coming down and the little breeze is shifting around with each shower. The watch on deck are shifting the yards around to catch each favouring breeze; probably it will end up with being calm entirely.

23rd November.
Across the Equator at last. A lot of sharks about today The boys caught two small ones and the deck stinks of fish like a fish market. However we will give them the credit of bringing the breeze we have got tonight and hope that the wind will be good to us now that we are in the North Pacific Ocean. We had quite a few kinds of fish about today. A lot were skipjacks, called so by the sailors because they skip out of the water when bigger fish chase them. Also a lot of jelly fish about, 8 or 10 feet long some of them, like snakes; coloured and spotted very prettily. There are a few birds about but they keep a long ways off.

Sunday November 28th.
Made a little progress this week, but not to boast of. We now have the NE Trade wind and hope it will carry us on our way to Japan. So far however they are 'Nowt to crack on' yet. We have passed the Caroline Islands without seeing any of them. It is now only about 2400 miles to Port from where we are and I hope to do it in about 28 days or less, if we should be in the least favoured when I lose these Trades.

Now we have had a little breeze it has not been so dreadfully hot, but if it falls calm again it will just be the same. The old French sailor I have who got his leg hurt six weeks ago is still unable to put his foot on the ground. I think the bone in his ankle got fractured but not broken clean through, so the leg will not heal up.

December 5th, 1897.
A fine breeze today, but wind and sea combined cause a very disagreeable motion on the part of the ship. But as we are going

along in the right way at a good speed, I do not mind it much. It is just a kind of reaction after a few days calm, so we want this to make up deficiencies. I am dull tonight and do not feel equal to writing more, so Goodnight My Dear.

December 12th, 1897.
We are now something less than 600 miles from Nagasaki but may easily be three weeks getting that distance, as the winds are likely to be unfavourable for us the rest of the way. We have had it right ahead from the NW for two days now, but it is getting a little better at present. We got a lot more damage done to some of our sails the other night, with a gale coming on us suddenly. However it might have been worse.

I am in hopes of getting to Port in under 10 days to keep the passage under 140 days and with fair play we should easily do it. It is like the little star that seems so near and yet so far. With a fair wind, three days would do us, but with a head wind, Oh so far away. The weather is getting cooler now; shoes and stockings, though not an absolute necessity, are just about comfortable. I fancy I am getting thin in the face, or it may be because I have my whiskers cut short, that makes me think my cheek bones are getting too prominent.

You will all be looking forward to Christmas coming and we are only hoping to get into Port before it gets here, otherwise we will be short of good Christmas roast beef and/or goose or turkey.

Sunday 19th December.
Well, we have worked our way a bit nearer Port but still we are not there. Yet have over 400 miles to go and a head wind to do it with. Our weather has been very changeable every day this week, either a gale or calm. The night before last, we had a fine fresh gale and sailed boldly up to within 5 miles of a very high Island (as high as Skiddaw). Just at midnight, it fell light and started going all round the compass and kept us for 12 hours till noon yesterday. We did not go a mile scarcely, or rather we just went backwards and forwards as the wind caught us ahead or astern. The eddy winds round the ends of the land caught us wherever we went, until just before noon, it came away a strong gale and we got away through

156

the Islands before dark.

Now we are becalmed again. A current has been helping us on our way considerably and just a few hours run would finish the passage before 140 days. I really feel I am getting thin, as I keep putting my hand up to my cheeks to feel how hollow they are. I can't say I feel my vest getting any slacker yet and I know I am not losing my appetite, only longing for a change of diet. Pea soup and salt pork I am heartily tired of, though after a month in Port we are glad of it for a change again. I think Willie is the tallest now of all the lads, but slender; he thinks we ought to be in harbour now.

Tuesday Dec. 21st 97.

We got up to the Port here at dark last evening and just dodged about in sight of the light all night, waiting for daylight. We managed to get in to anchor at 9 o'clock this morning, so we have accomplished the passage in less time than I expected, 139 days. Too soon for your letters, as there was not one for either of us from home. But the mail comes in again in a day or two, so they may come then. I was shocked and grieved to hear of Mr Ritson's death so very soon after we left. I have scarcely been able to think of anything but it all day.

They consider here that we have made a very good passage. At any rate, I am glad it is done with.

Fragment, no date.

.......proceed to Portland, Oregon, from here and must be there by April 30th. We have plenty of time to do it by then, without being favoured any. I think the other lads all got letters today. So Willie will likely be disappointed at being left out.

Nagasaki seems a queer little town. There are no houses on the streets, men do all the cab work and you would be amused to see a sturdy little Japanese running along with a huge perambulator on two wheels with me seated in it. I should think it was nearly as bad as holding me up on a bicycle. They get in between the shafts and keep up a regular trot the whole way. The little fellow that was trotting with me was quite an old man. The pilot told me he used to be the best runner in the town a few years ago. I noticed that nearly all the natives, though they had heavy clothing on, would all

Nagasaki harbour. These pictures were sent to Mary Messenger following the tragedy of 1898

have their necks and throats bare and little on their feet and the comical clogs they wear make them walk as if on stilts. They just have wooden soles, with thin pieces of wood two or three inches deep let in across the under side, like an ordinary miniature copystool. They secure across the foot with straps; they keep the wearer well up out of the mud at any rate. I will probably get you a pair to walk to school in before I leave here.

Give my love to all next door and at the Moor, I will write to them next when I get their letters. It has been very cold here today, with some snow or hail. Yesterday it was blowing very hard outside and they say the same here. It is a nice snug little Bay we are in and not at all like Valparaiso. But it is always very cold here in Winter and they say very hot in Summer.

With best love to yourself, I remain your loving father,
T. Messenger.

I forgot to say an enterprising Chinaman, 'throwing a sprat to catch a mackerel' if possible, made me a present of a very fine silk handerkerchief which may suit you, if I can save it till I get home again. He is a tailor and wants me to let him supply the sailors with clothes.

Nagasaki,   *January 1st, 1898.*

My Dear Daughter,
This is New Year's night and today I have not been on shore at all. It has been raining more or less continuously since last night. Most of my men are still ashore; Willie also has had his first run on shore today. It got out fine after dinner but did not hold up for long, so the boys would not have a nice walk.

Although I have been here nearly a fortnight, your letters have not yet come to hand. So unless your Uncle John has been mistaken about you having written, I can not make out where your letters have got to.

There has not been any great display of bell-ringing or firing of fireworks here to commemorate the New Year and it has been so wet that I have not troubled to fire a rocket myself.

The rain has at least brought much warmer weather with it, but they say here that they generally have a lot of snow in this month of January; I hope not this year. We are getting on very slowly discharging cargo; two days holiday this week and one last and more holidays to come.

So I am afraid we will be here nearly six weeks longer yet. I will send this letter by San Francisco boat on the 3rd and you will probably get it about the 8th or 10th of February.

There are lots of bicycles here in Nagasaki, but not many women about on them. There are no good roads for any distance and it is too hilly outside the town.

I have given that portrait of ours to a Japanese artist to copy it on silk and if he does it well I will have your Mother's likeness also painted on silk. I am also having the ship done too. So I am spending quite a lot of money here. I have got a fine camphor wood chest, which you may possibly take a fancy to, but I don't say you will get it. I suppose I must bring you a Japan tea set, warranted finest porcelain, from Japan. No doubt I could buy the things just as cheap in England.

There is always plenty of stir in the Bay here, with so many Men of War ships being in. There are 3 Russians, 1 American and a small British Gun Boat. So the place is alive with boats all day and night almost. Besides, a great number of steamers call here and passengers land here for an hour or two. Sandpan men, that is boatmen, are lying off with their boats waiting for chance passengers. I pay 75 cents for two boys and a sanpan a day, that is 18 pence English money. A rickshaw man costs the same; labour is very cheap here.

I think that I have walked round every part of the town now, as I generally take a walk in the afternoons, just to keep me from going to sleep on board and spoiling my nights rest. I had been told about going to see a Temple here, so I went with two Japs. But I was disappointed it did not amount to much, very little of it being left standing. But the walk was very good. The rain still comes down steadily but may be better tomorrow.

Sunday 2nd Jan.
It has been very fine today after the rain. The men who had liberty on shore have all come on board again now I think.

I just had a Captain Walker on board this evening with his wife and family for about half an hour. His father has that ship chandler's shop near Ritson's office. I think his wife is a foreigner, though not Japanese. They had five children with them, all girls, the eldest not 13. He says his son, a lad of 16, has gone home to Maryport.

As it is 11 o'clock, I will go to bed now and post this tomorrow. So with love to all, I remain ever your Father,   T. Messenger.

Nagasaki,   *January 10th, 1898.*

My Dear daughter,

I received your brief letter the day I posted my other one to you. I am pleased to see you were quite well, but a little sorry to see you had waited so long before writing and that that false report should have brought your letter to so sharp a conclusion. I judge you would be very much disappointed when you found out it was false. And just at that time, I myself was worrying about being delayed by a head wind and calms; about the first real stoppage I had had on the way.

I see you have been having some good long rides on your bike and evidently Miss H. must have got on to be a good rider too. I will surely have to get on and learn to ride, if only that I might keep you company on your journeys. But then I am afraid you would run away too fast for me, although I am thinking myself no end of a smart fellow.

We will be here for another month yet, as we are getting on very slowly at the cargo; we have only about 900 tons out yet and here three weeks. I have two or three men laid up nearly all the time and one in hospital. Another deserted, so we are a little short handed. The boys really stick to their work better than the men and have more spirit in them. The men are crying like so many big babies; wanting unlimited liberty to go on shore when they like, plenty of money and nothing to do. Also plenty of beef and tatties and grog. However, I just limit them in all things and let them cry.

I think that I have been pretty much all round the town now and will have to start seeing the country outside. Do you know that the Japanese are a very little race of people. The women are so very

A Nagasaki street circa 1898

short but extremely good-natured, laughing constantly and not at all bashful. The poor people's dress is just a big cloak, wrapped round them, with a belt in the middle and they all smoke a very mild tobacco in the tiniest of pipes made of brass. Just a whiff or two seems to please them.

I have been speculating in a tea set and other things, but I may sell them in Portland, if I can get a good price for them. Because if I bring them home, you would want another room to exhibit them. A dealer has decorated the mantle shelf with some ornaments and thinks I am going to buy them, but I hardly think I will; probably wait a while and inspect a sixpenny shop when I get home for cheap bargains. I think it amuses the lads to get these curio dealers into their place or on deck and examine their stock and probably hide some of it. Of course, things are too dear to buy anything.

A gentleman from the Dock Company here was on board today inspecting the Midas, as they are going to build a training ship for the Government here, to be about the same size or longer. So he was showing the Foremen about the ship to give them an idea of what things were for.

I have got a painting made of that photo of ours and he has copied you very well, but myself I do not think done well at all. He makes me too dark about the eyes and although I had him to alter it once, it is still too dark. I have given him your Mother's now, to see if he can do it any better.

With kind love to Aunt H. and your Grandparents and to yourself, I remain your loving Father,   *T. Messenger.*

(I hope you will write in time to Portland, soon after you receive this).

Barque Midas,   *Nagasaki Bay.*   *No date.*

My Dear Mary,

I am very pleased to tell you I have had a letter from you yesterday, also Uncle Tom. I was painting over the ships sides, when the Second Mate looked over and said, 'Billy, here is a letter for you. I was in such a hurry to get it, I climbed up and got it, then capsized the paint pot I think I read it through half a dozen times and I had such a good laugh to think of H. Pattinson talking. Esther would make half a dozen of her. Uncle has got your photo and his painted and yours is the best of the two. The artist has spoiled your father's somewhere. Father has got such a lot of curios here. He bought me a new suit here and it is very nice, so I am going to be a masher when I get back. I have begun to wear white shirts and your father likes to see me dressed up. He took me ashore with him to tea at Mrs Capt. Walker's two Sunday's ago. I was at church last Sunday with him and I stayed all day at Walker's, what a jolly time we had. They were aboard this afternoon for tea.

We are going out on Thursday we expect; I hope we may as I am about tired of being in here. Give my best love to Esther Graham when you see her.

The Midas is a lot better ship this voyage than she was last. Plenty to eat and everything you wish for. The crew gave three cheers for Uncle on his birthday.

And now I will say farewell to you with best love, I remain your affectionate and willing, loving Cousin,

W. Messenger.

Barque Midas,   *Nagasaki Harbour.*

(Written in circular fashion on very thin wood veneer)
January 16th 1898. Sunday 8.30 pm.
I am thinking, my dear daughter, you will not have had a letter written to you on such paper and in such a manner before. It is an idea just taken up this minute and already, as far as I have gone, I can not recommend the plan - or even the paper - to anyone else for its utility. The novelty may do for once in a while.

We are continually beset by all kinds of people offering all kinds of goods to our notice; some of it novel and curious but most of it second-rate and mediocre. Today, I was offered this paper made of wood and got some of it. It is not specially meant for writing in this manner; the idea, as I said before, is my own and it has just struck me further that it might be enlarged upon and it might also make a new industry. By leaving a small square of space in the centre for the writer to put in a small photo of himself or herself as the case might be. It would be so handy for young men writing to their best girls and vice versa, just to wind up with "Your Adorable" and stick in his photo. 10 years after, when the breach of promise case came in, he might repudiate the likeness and writing and so now, for that very reason, I will not put the idea on the market to make a fortune of it as I might have been tempted to do otherwise - and so ends this little piece of nonsense.

I have just let all the boys away to the town to a service this evening. The Chaplain has promised the men to come on board and hold a service in the Forecastle during the week and I hope it will be properly appreciated.

We are getting on very slowly with discharging and will be here another month yet, if not longer. The Doctors here are all agreed that the man I have in Hospital will never be any more use at the sea and I suppose the man will have to be sent home. Eventually he may be able for a watchmen's job or a light occupation. In any case, it is a bad job all round for the man and for the ship as well. I seem to be getting the cabin filled up with curios and paintings. The man has finished the one of your mother; I think, considering the photo being old, he has made a very good copy of it. The ship, he had got out of all proportion, so I had to send it back for him to make it all right. After that is done, I will have to stop spending money for needless articles.

I think I had the Forecastle clear of sick men for one day last week but another one was soon laid up again. The boys have all come on board again at half past nine; likely the streets are dark and empty, full of pitfalls to the unwary.

Monday 19th.
There is a mail leaving tomorrow via the Suez Canal and another leaves on Friday via San Francisco, which probably will be first at home. I went out on the railway the other day for a ride; it runs across to another Bay. You have to cross the Bay in a little steam launch and take the train the other side if you want to go further. From the station to the little landing place is a good distance, so we took a rickshaw, or rather the rickshawman wheeled us down; quite a long line of us, 20 people going along in single file and a rough road it was.

The Jap I was with took me to a native house to see a friend of his, a Japanese Doctor and there they treated us to tea (colourless) and fruit. The whole family were amused at my vain endeavours to pick up pieces of orange with chopsticks, that is two sticks a foot long which they use instead of knives and forks. It requires a little practice before one can manage to grip things firmly. Just as I thought I had a nice piece of orange ready to drop in my mouth, the sticks would separate and down it would drop. You see I dared not convey it to the mouth but lifted it and conveyed the mouth underneath it. When offering you anything, they bring it towards you, then kneel down and place it close to you. Anyone visiting the house, they don't shake hands with people as we do but kneel down and bow to the floor. The host does the same and they keep on repeatedly bowing to the earth. I got tired of bowing and so said, "Let us shake hands, old man, English fashion" and so I did and invited him to come on board and see me, though he could not speak a word of English. My interpreter said he asked me to come again and see them another day and he was sorry he had no tea to give me. They do not use sugar and milk in their tea. The Chaplain of the Home here was off with a gentleman and their ladies and we had a very nice service in the Forecabin. The ladies sang us "Where is my Wandering Boy Tonight". I think that we all enjoyed it very much.

With love to you all, I remain your Father,   *T. Messenger.*

Nagasaki,   *February 7th, 1898.*

My Dear Daughter,
Just by chance, your letter has caught us still here; only that we have been delayed by heavy rains from getting ballast, as we ought to have done. We would have been away to sea today, but now it appears as if we would not get away before Friday; this is only Monday.

I am very glad to see that you were quite well when you wrote. Had I not had this letter today, I was going to write to your Aunt H. Menhams to see if you were still in Crosby with them. I had Willie and Thomas and Burnett all at church with me yesterday forenoon. Mrs Walker took the boys to her house to tea and 7 o'clock dinner, but Willie will tell what an afternoon they had. I excused myself as I thought the boys would get on better if I was not with them. Mrs W. and family are all coming on board to tea tomorrow afternoon when they come home from school at 4 o'clock. Their Uncle, Captain R. Walker is here at present and will come with them. Not that we can entertain them much.

Next time you run to Allonby on your bike to see your Aunt and Uncle there, tell Uncle I only wish I could send him a few sticks more of the same tobacco. And tell him that those people who have lived here for 30 years or so, say that the Japanese are getting too saucy and independent since the war with China and they are just spoiling for a good licking. But all the same, I like them very well; they seem so happy and lighthearted and never in a hurry. When you go into their shops (they are all open in front and you walk right in through what appears to be the window), they will never tire showing off their wares, though you may not buy a cent's worth.

I will have to leave my old sailor that is in Hospital lame. He can not yet put foot to the ground and I am seriously afraid that in time his leg will have to be cut off. So he will be sent home to London on the 12th by the mail boat. Two of the men are on shore drunk today. I would have had them locked up but it is not worth while wasting money on them, as they will be sure to run away in Portland.

I hope by the time this reaches you, we will be very near to Portland and if you have not written before, you can write then at once. In no letters that Willie and I have received has any mention been made of Harry Gate, so we suppose he is quite well, but whether at home or in Africa we can not decide. Tell your Aunt, if she wants gold, now is the time to start off with a 'swag' for Klondyke. If she comes by way of Portland, I will help her on her way with biscuits and tinned meats. 40 years ago the cry was 'Bound for California'. Now it is 'Bound for Klondyke', to seek the shiny gold. I am far too old now, or I might run off myself to make a pile. I ought to have had it ready now, to be any good to me.

Tuesday
Well we have just had the Walkers on board to a cup of tea and they

Captain Robert Walker of Maryport
who taught the Japanese the art of shipbuilding. (Appendix D.)

have all gone on shore again now. Mrs W. spent most of her time talking to the boys about her son at Carlisle College. They have arranged that we come back from Maryport to Nagasaki again and they have talked so much about it that they really believe we are going to do so. Captain Walker and I had a good laugh at this painting of me in the bathroom. It is still there; I don't like to destroy it, such a valuable work of art. Possibly I might leave it and my blessing to your Aunt. Only I, I am afraid, appreciate and reverence it sufficiently. It seems Mr Marsh has not your own opinion of your wisdom and learning then. How many of you go for scripture and do you go in turns or alone. Mrs Walker made the Mate let the boys off a little earlier, for them to get cleaned and have a romp with the girls. She has five, one only two years old yet.

With love, I remain your Father,   *T. Messenger.*

AFTER MANY DAYS.

THE MISSING BARQUE MIDAS.

A dispatch dated Portland, August 10th, says:—What has every appearance of a genuine message from the lost barque Midas was found floating in the breakers off Stot's Place, about four miles north of the Columbia river Tuesday. The slip of paper was found in a bottle, and as far as it could be interpreted by handwriting experts the message reads as follows :—

"Brit. barque Midas, ballast shifted, all in small boats, first mate's boat capsized, will all drown——"

The Midas sailed from Nagasaki for Portland in January, 1898, with a crew of twenty-five men under charter to C. W. Tracy to load wheat. Soon after leaving the Japan coast a heavy storm swept over that region, and two other ships which afterwards reached Portland narrowly escaped foundering. On receipt of the message the signature was compared with that of Captain Messenger on his clearance papers at the Custom House. The resemblance is so striking as to leave small room for doubt as to its being made by the captain of the lost Midas.

A VALUABLE CARGO.

AFTER MANY DAYS.
THE MISSING BARQUE MIDAS.

A despatch dated Portland, August 10th 1898 says;

What has every appearance of a genuine message from the lost Barque 'Midas' was found floating in the breakers off Stot's Place, about 4 miles North of the Columbia river, Tuesday. The slip of paper was found in a bottle and as far as it could be interpreted by handwriting experts, the message reads as follows

"Brit. Barque Midas, ballast shifted, all in small boats. First Mate's boat capsized, will all drown....."

The Midas sailed from Nagasaki for Portland in January 1898, with a crew of 25 men, under charter to C W Tracy, to load wheat. Soon after leaving the Japan coast, a heavy storm swept over that region and two other ships, which afterwards reached Portland, narrowly escaped foundering. On receipt of the message, the signature was compared with that of Captain Messenger on his clearance papers at the Custom House. The resemblance is so striking as to leave small room for doubt as to its being made by the Captain of the lost Midas.

IN·MEMORY·OF·THE·

OFFICERS ✝ AND CREW

OF THE BARQUE "MIDAS".

WHICH WAS LOST WITH ALL HANDS.
DURING A PASSAGE FROM NAGASKI.TO PORTLAND.OREGON
LAST HEARD OF 14TH FEBRUARY.1898.

NAMES OF CREW.

CAPT,T.MESSENGER	A.B: O.W.SWAN
1ST MATE, R.RICHMOND	A.B: F. N. DAVIS
2ND MATE. G.H.JENKINS	A.B: T. ROSS
BOATSWAIN. A.THOMPSON	A.B: S. GORDON
CARPENTER. J.SHORT	A.B: J.COLLIGAM
STEWARD. J.T.ARMSTRONG	A.B: J.URRAY
COOK. L.S.JAMS	A.B; ADAMAMLING

A.B:E.SCOTT.

APPRENTICES

A.BURNETT	R.F.LIGHT
A.THOMAS	J.HOPKINS

W.MESSENGER.

Safe at anchor. now they rest with many of their best
but once again. they will set sail. their Saviour. Christ to meet

*Copy of the commemoration plaque erected in the Seamen's Mission,
Workington. Now in Maryport Maritime Museum*

APPENDIX A
COMMENTARY FROM THE
SEAFARING VIEWPOINT

by Roy Martin, ex Merchant Navy (Elder-Dempster Line, Anchor Line, Currie Line, Shell Tankers, British and Burmese Steam Navigation Company)

Preface Captain Bligh. . . Despite his extreme behaviour in the 'Bounty', his reputation as a seaman and navigator was second to none.

Introduction Minor gaps. . . Ships officer jobs could be sporadic due to dry-docking, refitting, slack trade or perhaps the individual had offended the owner or superintendent.

Clothes washing. . . Fresh water was in very short supply. Salt water produced little lather and needed much scrubbing; rain showers were useful to swill clothes.

17.8.93 Dunboyne of Dublin. . . Shrewd of owner Mr. Ritson to register the ship in Eire.

27.8.93 Dogwatch. . . 4pm to 6pm (1st), 6pm to 8pm (2nd).

14.9.93 Veer(ing). . . To shift wind direction clockwise (Northern hemisphere), anti-clockwise (Southern hemisphere).

5.11.93 Guano. . . Bird droppings, used for early fertiliser. The least favourite cargo because of tics and ammonia smell.

27.5.94 Holystone. . . This was the sailor's most grievous task. It involved pushing back and forth along the deck a lump of pumice stone, about the size of half a breeze block, whilst kneeling. Cold salt water was freely available as a lubricant and dispersant. Sand was used under the holystone for particularly difficult areas. The work was back-breaking, soul-destroying and the effect on the knees was spectacular. The task was often used as a punishment. It was common to have a chorus or even a fiddler to keep time. In the R.N. a rope's end would keep attention the task; in the M.N. the Bosun's boot.

'Holystone. . . A Sailor's Poem'.
Seven bell's were made. . .
The watch came from below. . .
To bend the knee and neck. . .
But not in prayer, . . .
But to curse and swear. . .
And holystone the deck.

14.6.94 Fastnet. . . gunfire. Explosive charges were detonated to enable ships to identify a Lighthouse. Each signal was unique to that location.

22.8.94 Smart passage. . . Very much the concern of sailing ship Captains. Owners did not appreciate over-careful masters. They wanted quick voyages, hence quicker returns on their money. Captain Messenger obviously wondered about the capability of the Ladas as a fast ship and his ability to get the best out of her. It was usual with new crews to feel that their previous ship was best until the current vessel was tested well either by the weather or rapid passages. Some ships gained awful reputations and were seen as 'jinxed', especially if men were lost whilst working ship.

25.8.94. Pitch. . . Pitch tar on the deck is very deceptive in hot weather. It is not very hot to touch until you stand on it in your bare feet; much shouting and dancing about occurs!

1.9.94. Madeira. . . Means 'wood' in Portugese. It was a heavily wooded island which had more or less permanent forest fires. It was therefore easily identified from afar by the smell of the wood smoke.

6.9.94 Peak of Teneriffe (Pico de Teide). . . This is a very distinctive volcano shape. It is a welcome sight for ships in either direction. It can be sailed around using a sextant angle, so with a bearing or two you have a good positional fix.

6.9.94 Afternoon. . . Always enjoyed by watch-keepers because of 'getting your head down', usually in some comfort. Not enjoyed by those standing the 12 to 4 (graveyard) watch.

10.9.94 Stiff collars. . . A great nuisance at sea because of the irritation. Tended to give rise to crops of boils, especially in adolescent apprentices. Rice water was used as starch.

30.9.94 Ship. . . Sailing vessel square rigged on all masts, whereas the Barque Ladas had less sail area.

30.10.94 Ice. . . Life got very difficult in enclosed waters with poor visibilty, ice and small islands. Presumably there was very little detail on charts at this time. He would be using his own journal and/or a 'Pilot Manual'. There was great danger of being driven by wind and tide onto a lee shore; hence his need to 'stand off' away from the shore and zig-zag (tack) westward into clearer water.

6.11.94 Worst tricks. . . A ship can develop a very odd motion which is not predictable. The stern lifts high out of the water with a corkscrew motion; at masthead 360 degrees may be described, often at terrifying speed, then ratcheting in the opposite direction. Much water is taken on board during pitching, rolling and corkscrewing; nobody knows where the next heavy sea is coming from. People get injured or swept away. Steering is a nightmare; very heavy dangerous work.

26.12.94 Christmas. . . A sad time for sailors generally, especially if you are stuck up some backwater. The lads tend to go amok slightly. (Our ship was abandoned for 11 days in Hamburg over Christmas).

20.1.95 Rails. . . The main export of the iron and steel industry in

West Cumberland. New railways in many parts of the world ran on Cumbrian rails.

24.3.95 Days work. . . Refers to the title of the notebook kept by navigators, hence 'Dayswork' (a personal record).

25.3.95 Albatross. . . Taking these birds was considered very bad luck and much frowned upon. Legend says that albatrosses contained the souls of drowned sailors.

14.4.95 (Sunday). Reported. . . It was very important that the location and condition of a ship was reported to the agent in the Port of Destination, hence to its owners.

16.4.95 (Tuesday). Breezes blow onto the shore in the evening and off shore in the morning. The ability of the Ladas to sail into the wind seemed better than most ships.

5.5.95 Laying over. . . Whilst waiting for cargo. Often a magical time for sailors to 'go walkabout' if allowed. (I ran with gauchos, trail herding up the Rio de la Plata).

May 95 People. . . Ships agents/chandlers. Paperwork such as bills of lading, clearance papers and ships supplies.

Cheating. . . It was very common for sailors, come easy, go easy, to be readily swindled by their representatives in these deals e.g chandlers, publicans, pimps, 'con' men, or even one of their colleagues.

26.5.95 10 o'clock has rung. An odd remark for a sailor, The usual style was '4 bells were made', never rung. Perhaps a translation for his daughter.

8.6.95 It was the custom for ships below the Equator to have a sharks tail fin lashed to the bowsprit end, as a good omen.

25.6.95 Legend says that if a shark's heart is cut out it will beat until

sunset. We caught many sharks – very exciting and highly dangerous – but never witnessed the legend.

4.7.95 Dolphin catching was not favoured. Sailors looked upon
them as lucky and good.

Sun. 7.7.95 Log. . . A quadrant of wood with a three rope harness,
one to each corner. One leg was removed by a trip line when a timed
number of knots had passed through your hands.12.7.95.   The
burden of being Captain. Very few would share their worries and
concerns. Many kept detailed written log-books of their thoughts
and observations. Many took to drink.

14.7.95 Getting short of water and stores was a feature of many
ships. Often due to bad management and fiddling rather than
adverse waether.

27.7.95 Washed out. . . Deck planking shrank massively when dried
out. Pitch melted and oakum failed. The deck then became like a sieve.

9.8.95 Money. . . This was called an 'Allotment'. Written out by the
sailor and signed by him, the agent was honour-bound to pay.

7.10.95 Cleaned. . . Referring to the ship's bottom. Barnacles and
weed grow quickly on a ship which is not moving. Special 'anti-
fouling' was very toxic (now banned).

8.12.95 Laying over. . . It is very difficult to sleep, even today, when
ships roll like a pendulum. After several days of this, extreme
tiredness sets in. (We used to retreat to hammocks in bad weather).

19.1.96 Sails off the ship. . . It could be too dangerous to put a man
aloft; there would be much flogging of heavy canvas, sheets and
halyards and footing could easily be lost.

26.1.96 Ship's paint. . . Was made on board from linseed oil and lead
pigments. It was a tedious but quite skilled task.

2.2.96 Flying fish. . . dart and swoop at very high speeds. They are beautiful to watch but seem to lose their colour when caught.

14.4.96 Parallel rules. . . Difficult without them so the Carpenter would no doubt make a new set. They were very skilled craftsmen.

19.4.96 Strange bird. . . May be a secretary bird

26.4.96 Barque like the Dutch Barque. . . Sailing ships can be identified at a distance by the profile of rigging, masts and sails e.g. the 'cut of the jib', even if the hull was below the horizon.

31.5.96 Boy's house. . . Where the apprentices lived, usually four of them. Situated on the main deck, also called the half-deck. If the doors were open on both sides the sea could sweep them or their belongings out.

21.6.96 Life boat. . . tackles. Lifeboats were lashed to the deck with wooden chocks and covered over. The rope tackles (pulleys) had to be set up if the boat was required. On a bad ship, it was not unknown for the boat to be dried out and leaking and sometimes stuck immovably to the deck with paint.

28.6.96 Point of the compass. . . There are 32 points, which divided into 360 degrees, means that each point is just over 11 degrees. These may be further sub-divided into quarter points. Sailing ships can only sail at an angle across the wind. Sailing is most efficient the closer to the wind you can get without endangering the ship. Some ships could sail closer to the wind than others.

6.7.96 Lee shore. . . The ship is caught by the wind blowing on to the shore and can not sail to seaward to avoid the hazards of the coastline. It is the sailor's worst dream. The same applies when a power-driven ship breaks down.

19.7.96 Ware or Waring ship. . . A voice command to turn her round sharply. May come from Beware.

26.7.96 Clothes. . . Mildew and fungus arrives at an amazing rate. Spare second-hand clothes were kept in the 'slop chest' and sold to the crew. Used also for stowaways and rescued survivors.

2.8.96 Electric light. . . Known as St. Elmo's fire. Resembles silver tinsel or frost in a fridge. Eerie and spectacular to see.

16.8.96 Slip overboard. . . We were once discharging off-shore at Accra in Ghana, which is well known for its rollers and surf. We unloaded the President of Liberia's new Cadillac into a large catamaran barge, which promptly rolled over into the surf, causing the vehicle to disappear.

Bethel ship . . . Probably an early version of the Missions to Seamen, also known as The Flying Angel.

30.8.96 English people. . . I generally found expatriates as Capt. Messenger did. They definitely felt a cut above the rest and were reluctant to leave the English compound. They certainly did not want to rub shoulders with the average sailor.

Sept. 96 Catch a 'crab'. . . Catching the water out of rythm with the rest of the oarsmen, therefore inefficient rowing. Required some practice to get a boat's crew pulling as an entity. A source of some competition between ships.

24.1.97 Whistling buoy. . . An interesting device, consisting of a tube attached vertically to a floating buoy, one end of the tube being in the water. As the water level varies, so does the air level, producing a mournful whistling which was very difficult to miss.

14.2.97 Thunder. . . jubilant. Wonderful use of language. Imagine an iron ship, steel rigging, possibly steel masts; the whole thing therefore like tuning fork. In a thunderstorm there could be a cataclysmic noise, with foam blowing and hissing and wind shrieking through the rigging. The rigging hums and throbs, the yards creek, the gear strains, the metal plates groan and rivets crack. Lightning flashes crack and sizzle. It is an elemental feeling.

15.2.97 Drop on deck. . . Very easy to lose your footing when descending wet or tarred rigging on a rolling ship. It was simple to miss the last 'ratline' as your body weight hurtles downward when the ship rolls downwards.

21.2.97 Frightened the wind. . . Evidently superstition was still prominent in the sailor's mind.

7.3.97 Ropes. . . through the ports. 'Washports'; rectangular ports through the bulwark (wall round the ship). Often had a hinged flap to let water off the ship but retrieving trailing ropes and lines through this was a job.

8.3.97 Soundings. . . Lead weights are used for soundings. They have a concave bottom end which is plugged with grease. When it hits the bottom, sand, shells, stones etc. stick to it so you can identify what is under you. Modern charts show the nature of the sea bottom. Capt. Messenger would have recorded his findings in his journal; obviously he referred to it as a comparison voyage by voyage. Pilot manuals for all seas, oceans and coasts are now covered by the British Admiralty, the U.S.A., Norway or Germany. They are very accurate and constantly revised.

21.3.97 Made snug. . . the sails. Reducing the amount of sail and securing it well. Often referred to as 'under bare poles', with very strong storm sails set to keep the ship steady and steerable.

Coal hole. . . A small bunker below deck, either side of the galley. Held the coal for the galley range and cabin and saloon fires (rarely lit).

Sea sick. . . Interesting that an old seaman complained of sea-sickness. It must have been a very odd motion of the ship, caused by wind, tide and current in unusual combination. This could be common over the Dogger Bank in the North Sea.

4.4.97 Queenstown. . . May be the old name for Cobh, across Cork harbour.

Willie. . . chief helmsman. Indicates increasing ability and confidence in Willie. 1) He was chosen as the day helmsman 2) He obviously had grown taller and stronger to handle the heavy steering, which often had unpredictable kick-back which could cause serious injury. 3) He needed to read the compass, which would have been in quarter points. Willie had to keep the ship steady, track as straight as possible and keep the wind in the sails. Sails draw best when they are very slightly curved and taut. This could be very hard at night, but you can hear the sail and rigging noises; you feel the ship balanced on the rudder.

11.4.97 Doldrums. . . Area of light winds and calm/oily seas near the Equator. The atmosphere and lack of progress could mean grumbles, quarrels and frayed tempers.

2.5.97 Tarring. . . This was really unpleasant, dirty work. Usually done with a wad of rag dipped into Stockholm tar and wiped into each strand of wire rigging. Necessary to grease the hand before, otherwise the skin was irritated. A Bosun's chair was used to slide down near-vertical rigging – which was quite exciting.

30.5.97 Lighten ship. . . The River Shannon is a broad but shallow estuary. It was common practice to off-load parcels of cargo to lessen the draft of the ship to clear the river bottom at lowest tide.

Aug. 97 Tuskar. . . Tuscar, a rock.

Sept.19th 97 Tristan da Cunha. . . A British dependency, formerly Portugese; the remainder of a British garrison. The people have a strong Devonian accent. The island receives two supply ships a year from Cape Town, about a 1000 miles away. They are still run by Messrs. Curwen and Co., old West Country shipowners. (I visited there in 1953, on the S.S. Tectarius from the Persian Gulf to Buenos Aries, with mail and medical supplies. We couldn't go alongside so surf boats came out. We met the

Head Man, William Repeto, and received the impression that Tristan was a time capsule. I think there are a similar number of people still there).

26.9.97 Greenwich Meridian and Prime Meridian are one and the same. The Cape of Good Hope is about 18 degrees East.

1.1.98 Sandpan/sanpan. . . I don't know this term but perhaps it is a precursor of sampan, which is a small sailing boat, usually sculled over the stern (propelled with one hand).

APPENDIX B
MARYPORT AND WEST
CUMBERLAND.

In 1974, Local Government reorganisation amalgamated Cumberland and Westmorland into the County of Cumbria.

Although the Romans established a significant settlement, as evident in the town's Roman Museum, until the 18th century Maryport was a village named Ellen Foot, at the mouth of the River Ellen. The Industrial Revolution changed all that, for the area was blessed with coal, iron ore and enterprise. Local land-owner Humphrey Senhouse was behind the building of the docks and the town was named after his wife. Shipping, ship-building, fishing, coal mining and iron founding were its staple industries and the export trade steadily grew to rival that of Liverpool, although the population was never much above 12,000. The town also has Titanic connections as the birthplace of Thomas Ismay, founder of the White Star Line.

Later a steel works was established at Workington 6 miles down the coast. Since the 19th century, it specialised in making rails which also become a prime export, supplying many of the World's developing railways. It continues making rails today.

Whitehaven is also mentioned in the book. A few miles south of Workington, this is another interesting old town with a proud maritime tradition. It has the honour of being the only town in Britain ever to be attacked by an American warship.

Unfortunately with the decline of coal and changes in the steel industry and world trade generally, the West Cumberland area suffered badly, especially in the depression of the 1930's; in that sense Maryport is a shadow of its former self.

However West Cumbrians are nothing if not adaptable and Maryport has benefited by grants from Europe and other sources. The harbour area has been opened up and landscaped. It is a now a flourishing marina for sea-going yachts from many parts, with residential areas, a fine marine aquarium and a fascinating maritime museum. However its 18th century charm has been preserved. Despite the industrial legacy, the attractive area north of Maryport is designated as being of Special Scientific Interest. The Solway estuary is an important focal point for birdlife and the English Lake District and Border Country lie a short distance away.

APPENDIX C
CORRESPONDENCE WITH PORT
OF STOCKHOLM

Your ref.   Our ref.   Stockholm

                              Harbour Master   May 18th, 1998
                              T Krokstedt/GK

Dear Sir,

The of Chapman, ex Dunboyne

Thanking for your inquiry we hereby gladly wish to inform that the above mentioned ship still is going strong and sticks to her mooring/berth at the Skeppsholmen shore.

The ship has been seen at her berth for nearly fifty years and is a natural eye-catcher, white against the greenery and ancient buildings of the island Skeppsholmen as seen from the Old Town.

The ship is in a good state of repair, considering her age.

The ship is used as a youth hostel administrated by the Swedish Tourist Association. We hereby enclose some pictures taken on May 13th this year and a cut out from the Swedish chart 6141, Port of Stockholm where the af Chapman is shown as any other fixed object at her berth along the western shore of Skeppsholmen.

                    Yours sincerely,

                    PORT OF STOCKHOLM
                    Operations dep/staff

                    Thomas Krokstedt

PORT OF STOCKHOLM

Magasin 3, Frihamnen   VAT.no.: SE556008164703
P.O.Box 27314   Tel: +46 - 8 - 670 26 00   Bank giro: 720-0306

APPENDIX D
CAPTAIN ROBERT WALKER AND
THE MITSUBISHI CONNECTION

Captain Robert Walker of Maryport, who is mentioned in the Nagasaki chapter, was employed by the Japanese to advise them on building sailing ships. Captain Walker was in command of the Japanese sailing ship 'Niigata-Maru' when on March 11th 1878 she sailed from Yokohama arriving in London, the first Japanese ship to do so. New engines were installed and her gross tonnage increased to 1910. Having sailed from Japan as a sailing ship, she returned to Yokohama arriving on November 25th 1878 as a steamer.

On the voyage were students of the Mitsubishi Institute of Mercantile Marine, now Tokyo University of Mercantile Marine, using the journey as a training exercise in all aspects of seamanship.

Captain Walker married a Japanese lady. They had five children and on a visit to Maryport she died, her body being buried at the town's cemetery.

Captain Walker was related to William Walker, one-time Ship Builder, Repairer and Chandler of Maryport.

APPENDIX E
EARLY LETTERS

Written before and after my Aunt and I paid a visit to friends who lived on a farm at Arley on the Severn.

Ship "Dunboyne"   *Barry Dock, 1890.*

My Dear Daughter,

I suppose you will be at home again by this time and ready for school again. We are now under the tips and getting coke put into us but whether they will fill the ship right up or not, I can not say. If they do, we will get away this weekend sometime. It was very stormy and rainy last night and laid all the coal dust for us. This morning was fine but came on rainy in the forenoon. The Captain's wife and baby and her Aunt have come to Barry and they are going to take the infant with them this voyage, so we will have more music than from the bird.

I did not get into Birmingham on Monday night util half past twelve. I got taken round by Dudley and as our train was to start at 12.15, I thought I had missed it. However it did not start until 1.15, so I had some time to wait and it stopped a good while in Kidderminster. So I need not have gone to Birmingham at all, only I was afraid it would not.

Wednesday   *1890.*

My Dear Mary Adelaide,

I am going to leave here for London tonight, but will call at Birmingham on my way to see the Martindales and may stop there until Monday if they are not crowded with visitors. So if Aunt Hannah is ready to come, she could meet me there. The Steward has made some toffee for you today and I have to bring it. I may easy eat it on my way or lose it, then you will be disappointed.

The ship is going to lay here until 10th July, so I will have about 3 weeks holiday and no task. Is Saturday a Carlisle trip day, or a Maryport one? I will hardly get from Martindales before Monday.

Dunboyne, Barry Dock.   *1890.*

My Dear Sister and Daughter,
I take it for granted that you are at Arley or Bromley by this time and hope you have had better weather than we have had this last two days. Regular wintry it has been with us here.

I have had no word from Crosby this week yet, so I don't know if Sir Wilfred has been beaten or not.

We are made fast in the middle of the dock and expect to go in for our stiffening, that is what coals we are going to take, then we will get our ballast out ready for loading.

There are a lot of very big ships here in this dock and I am just thinking that if I can not get to see you, you may come down here and see me if you can stop away so long. I have not seen Mr Molineux in Cardiff, only the first night I was there the Stewards wife was in and they sent word for me to call up again. The other brother from Barry is still up in Cumberland yet so I believe, unless he has come home since Sunday.

I don't get on shore much here though it is very nice round about the place. I had a good walk round on Sunday night and came to the conclusion that the Welsh girls are rather pretty, or I was helped to that conclusion by the young man with me.

I trust Belle and husband and also Sally and hers are all quite well and that you are enjoying yourselves.

I remain, you Brother,   *T. Messenger.*

Dunboyne, Barry Dock, Thursday.   *1890.*

Dear Hannah,
We are ready for cargo and waiting our turn and if the ship in turn before us is not ready, we may get in a little sooner then we

expected and, consequently, away a little sooner. So that perhaps it would be a pity for to disturb you, when you are comfortable, to bring you down here for a few days where everything is smothered in coal dust. M.A. does not say when you intend to go back home but perhaps you had not settled any time to go back and are waiting for me.

The Captain is going home tomorrow for a few days and I will not be able to get away, so you had better make the most of your time while at Mrs Martindales and not be too much disappointed that I can not get to see you. If at any time I find I can run up before you go home, I will do so. I did not get Mary's toffee sent yesterday, so will send it today and I am sure Janie and the other children about there will appreciate it. He spoiled the first panful yesterday when making it but he assures me this lot is all right. I have not tried it; I ate too much of what was spoiled!

Elizabeth tells me they had a most enjoyable trip to the Isle of Man, none of them sick, but the old Carpenter was not there. Tell Janie, I am sorry I was not there to take a back seat in that ride through the Forest of Bewdley. But then you know I walked it and when I think of it, I get in a state of perspiration all over from the heat. I am writing this in a hurry as I am expecting the surveyor to come any minute to survey the ship and see she is in a fit state to carry coke to Australia. There are a good many loading for the same place, Port Pirie, but freights are very low.

With kind love to you all, I remain, Your Brother, *T. Messenger.*

Wed. June 17th 1891.   *Ship off Hastings.*

My Dear Daughter,
Here we have got nearly home after a favourable passage so far of 120 days. We have had light winds and calms for the last 9 days or we would have been up before. The owners will likely have sent you word that we were near at hand as we were signalled some few days ago. We have just had some little entertainment; a steamboat full of people came alongside and the band struck up "Garry Owen" but it was only weak as the band only consisted of a

clarionet but they gave us a lot of papers on board.

We are likely to be 3 or 4 days getting to Hull yet, as the wind is very light and we have about 300 miles to go yet but I hope we will get up Friday or Saturday. I am glad to say that I have been in the very best of health all the passage and so has all else but the Second Mate had his leg broken by a sea two months ago and is only now getting able to be out on deck with help.

Hoping that you are all well at Birkby Moor and Crosby, with Kind love to all, I remain, your Father,

T. Messenger.

Thursday Morning, 4 o'clock.
Just anchored in the Downs, to get a North Sea Pilot from Deal and we will start again in a couple of hours.

Ship Dunboyne.   *Hull. 10.7.1891.*

My Dear Daughter,
I received your letter this morning and shall be very sorry if I have to disappoint you next week again. But I may very likely have to do so.

We are going from, here to Middlesborough to load a cargo of coke and pig iron for Port Pirie in South Australia and we will likely not get away from here before next Saturday. So I do not see that I can get home before we get to our other Port. It will just take us a day; it is about 30 miles this side of Newcastle. So when I get there I shall be so much nearer home.

I am glad Jane got the order all right. Am in hopes to be home before your Band of Hope trip as we are more likely than not to be at sea by that time. They will soon put coke in the ship, should they be ready for us. We are now in the dry dock and will stop here until Monday. The Captain is at home; he will come back again on Monday and then I think he will have the Steward back to go round with the ship.

I feel very tired and sleepy tonight, so must close, with kind love from your loving father,   *T. Messenger.*

ACKNOWLEDGEMENTS

I would like to express grateful thanks to all those who have helped see this project to fruition, including;

My wife Barbara, for her patience.

Roy Martin of Preston, for the seafaring viewpoint.

Lucy Barnes of Blackburn, for helping to check the manuscript.

Gary Marsden of Chester, for supporting my meagre computer literacy, especially through hard disk failure and virus invasion.

Should anyone perusing the Cumbrian Archives wish to delve further into the story of the Messengers, stirling work has already been done by Barbara Riding of Blackburn. I am indebted to Mrs. Riding, a friend of my mother's, who took a great interest in the letters after my father died. She became so involved that she was moved to do some research into Tom Messenger's background, with the help of friends in Cumbria. I would like to thank all who helped her to do this, in particular Mary and Walter Bell; Mrs. Bell worked with my mother and her grandparents bought Birkby Moor from the Messengers. Barbara Riding has used the material to enlighten and enthrall people on lecture circuits from church groups to historial societies.